HISTORIC TALES

of Cashiers

NORTH CAROLINA

HISTORIC TALES

of

Cashiers

NORTH CAROLINA

JANE GIBSON NARDY

THE
History
PRESS

Published by The History Press
Charleston, SC 29403
www.historypress.net

First published 2008
Second printing 2011

ISBN 9781540229243

Library of Congress Cataloging-in-Publication Data

Nardy, Jane Gibson.
Historic tales of Cashiers, North Carolina / Jane Nardy.
p. cm.
Includes bibliographical references.
ISBN 9781540229243
1. Cashiers (N.C.)--History--Anecdotes. 2. Cashiers (N.C.)--Biography--Anecdotes. I.
Title.
F264.C266N37 2008
975.6'95--dc22
2008013744

For Jean, my best friend since we were twelve years old. Thanks for all your help.

CONTENTS

CONTENTS

HISTORY SPEECHES

PREFACE

A lifetime of love for my ancestral home, Cashiers, North Carolina, led to the writing of these true tales. Through the years, my personal library of several generations of family pictures, letters, memorabilia, deeds, wills and more has grown. Fortunately, I descend from pack rats who are deemed clutter bugs by those who prefer a perfectly kept house to old faded scrapbooks or a lock of their great-grandmother's hair pressed in the pages of a Bible. But I have always known that a pack rat is a historian's best friend.

This book contains a collection of diverse stories covering a wide range of subjects, all with a connection to the Cashiers, North Carolina area. I am a direct descendant of the founding family of Cashiers—the Zacharys. Although I was not born in Cashiers, I grew up in a home in Atlanta built by my grandfather Zachary, who, after graduating from Teacher's Normal in Cullowhee in 1899, moved to Georgia to teach school. Throughout my childhood, both in Atlanta and on visits to Cashiers, I was constantly hearing stories about Cashiers and my many kinfolk there. Each year at the annual Zachary reunion at the Lower Zachary Cemetery in Cashiers, the large group ate food and told stories about departed loved ones.

This constant exposure to the history of family and place led me into a career as a certified professional genealogist, where genealogy and history seamlessly blended. My permanent move to Cashiers in 1990 provided the chance to focus my research on all things Cashiers. My mother's mountain childhood friend and cousin, Madge Dillard Merrell, asked me to start writing down her remembrances so they wouldn't be lost, and so I did.

As one of the founders of the Cashiers Historical Society, I was offered the opportunity to put my knowledge of Cashiers Valley's past to good use. From the large volume of old letters written in the 1800s and 1900s, one could find vivid descriptions of what mountain life used to be like. For the historical society, I wrote a few newspaper articles and started designing and leading history tours around Cashiers and giving talks on Cashiers history at various locations. From original Cashiers store account books, marriage registers at the courthouse, tombstones in the cemeteries, ragged old newspaper clippings and many other sources, the rhythm of yesteryear is being partially reconstructed. Add to all that the memories currently being collected from descendants of the old local families, plus recollections from early tourists and summer folks, and you have material enough for volumes.

Since 2005, I have written a monthly Cashiers history article for the *Mountain Laurel Magazine* and many of those will be found in this book. The tales are divided into four sections—A Mixed Bag of Tales, From the Memory of Madge Dillard Merrell, Selected Zachary Stories and finally, History Speeches.

A Mixed Bag of Tales

MERRY TALES FROM
CAMP MERRIE-WOODE

We have all heard about Camp Merrie-Woode—its beautiful location on Fairfield Lake with a view of Old Bald Mountain, its top national rating and its listing on the National Register of Historic Places. Now, let us hear a firsthand account from one of the Merrie-Woode alumni on the camping experience in the earliest days.

In 1926, when Merrie-Woode had been in business less than a decade, a little ten-year-old girl by the name of Frank Schoolfield spent the first of her three summers at the camp. She was accompanied only by her older sister, Lazora, and the journey to the mountains started when they boarded the train at their hometown of Danville, Virginia. The sisters changed trains at Spartanburg, South Carolina, and took off on the last leg of the train trip, which would end at the Lake Toxaway spur station. There, they were met by either a Fairfield Inn representative or a staff member of Camp Merrie-Woode and whisked away for their two-month adventure. Naturally, Frank experienced homesickness that first summer.

Frank Schoolfield Jordan, who is today usually in residence at her home in the Cashiers High Hampton Colony, remembers, with affection, many details of her camp days. Summers were cool in the mid-1920s, and the girls dressed accordingly in gray wool midi-blouses, green pleated bloomers and stockings. They lived in small chestnut bark cabins that were

Camp Merrie-Woode, taken from Fairfield Lake. *Camp Merrie-Woode Collection.*

referred to as "shacks" and had names like "Nut Shell," "Linger Longer," "Chug-A-Wump" and "Sunny Shack." The routine of the day started with rising at 6:00 a.m., a quick dip in the lake and raising the flag, all before breakfast. At meals, it wasn't required to eat everything on the plate, but the girls were encouraged to at least eat three spoonfuls of each thing served.

Campers came from many places, including Atlanta, Birmingham and Richmond. According to their ages, the girls were called "Pages," "Squires," "Yeomen" or "Knights." For a special treat, the "Knights" were sometimes allowed to row across the lake to Fairfield Inn. Some of the favorite activities were hiking to the top of Old Bald Mountain or into Panthertown Valley and going by horseback from the camp, up through the saddle between Rock Mountain and Chimney Top Mountain, then down into Whiteside Cove, through Horse Cove and ending up in Highlands—all on dirt roads..

Frank remembers that both the director, Dammie Day, and her assistant, Mary Turk, were strict and kept a close watch over their campers. Most of all, Frank remembers how wonderful everything was in those early Camp Merrie-Woode summers.

REMEMBERING
ETRULIA RICE WHITE

In Cashiers, where Wendy's now serves up hamburgers, there used to stand a house in which Etrulia Rice White and her family lived. Etrulia, born in 1920, was the youngest of the nine children of William Stephen Rice and Rosetta Crow, members of the large, close-knit Rice family of the Bull Pen area. In 1936, when Etrulia was in her mid-teens, she married Ernest White and they first lived on Heady Mountain Road, where their two eldest children were born. Ernest initially made his living as a logger, but later in life he worked as a heavy equipment operator. A few years after their marriage, the Whites moved to a house on Highway 64, near the intersection of Slabtown Road. In 1950, they moved to another house on Highway 64, a little closer to the crossroads. It sat about where the Smokehouse Restaurant sits today, just across the little creek from Wendy's. The family's final move involved physically moving the house itself across the creek to the current Wendy's location and adding rooms to the structure, plus building a one-car detached garage. About the time of the relocation of the house, the White's last child and only girl, Ellen, was born at the Highlands Hospital. She was the only one of the five children not born at home.

Each year, Etrulia planted a garden to provide her family with fresh vegetables. Any surplus was canned and stored in the basement for winter use. In addition to raising her five children, she worked most of her life for

Etrulia Rice White. She was born in the Bull Pen area and lived her adult life in Cashiers. *Ellen White Stewart.*

summer people in the capacity of housekeeper. For more than twenty-five years, Mrs. Ernestine Noe McKee Pope employed Etrulia, who Ernestine called "Trulie," and the two became fast friends and companions. They were quite a pair—Ernestine, tall and stately, and Etrulia, a petite lady speaking with the beautiful, fast-disappearing mountain accent. At Christmas, Etrulia would go into the woods, gather galax, trailing arbutus and dog hobble and make lovely holiday arrangements for her clients.

Except for the last eighteen months of her life at Fidelia Eckerd Nursing Home, Etrulia lived out her old age in her own home with the loving care of her children. It was a life well lived, filled with hard work and dedicated service to others. Remember her when you drive into Wendy's.

APPLE BLOSSOM TIME
IN CASHIERS VALLEY

The Western North Carolina Mountains have always had a favorable climate for growing fine apples, and one of the first things planted after the pioneers cleared their land was an apple orchard. In a little over ten years after the Zachary family had arrived in Cashiers Valley, we find the first written record of apple trees in the store account book of Alexander Zachary. Besides recording the names of the customers at his store and listing the merchandise they were buying, he periodically made mention of the activity in his apple groves.

March 31, 1845	
Grafted Buffs Upper Row	*130*
Never Fails Low Row	*25*
Limber Twigs Low Row	*12*
Yellow Skins—Winter	*26*
Yellow Skins—Summer	*15*

In 1847, through 1851, Alexander continued listing varieties of apples he was either planting or grafting until there was a grand total of twenty-one varieties mentioned. Considering the phonetic spelling of the time, these are some additional names of the apples: Howards; English

T.R. Zachary and his second wife, Mary Rogers Zachary, at their Cashiers farm. One of his occupations was selling seedling apple trees to area farmers. *Jane Gibson Nardy.*

Crabs; Granny; Green Pippins; Morgans; World's Wonder; Junaluska Valley; Streeked; Red; Horse; Roiel Paremains; Buckinghams; Northern Red Winter; Knox; and Harvey.

Apples were important to mountain survival for two main reasons: first, they were important as food for the family that could be prepared in a variety of ways and preserved for winter eating; and second, they were important as a cash-producing crop. As Dr. James M. Zachary wrote in his 1880 letter:

> *We have but little money here. The reason is that we do not use it for currency* [but] *my taxes was* [sic] *about $85 and it was all I could do to get it up without leaving home and go off and work for it.*

Hauling a wagon full of apples to the autumn markets in South Carolina could provide real currency for a man to pay his taxes and buy items he couldn't grow or produce, such as coffee, sugar, flour and store-bought shortening like Crisco.

Many apple farmers used a unique method of making apple harvesting easier. The limbs of a young apple tree were weighted down with rocks to keep them from growing straight up. That way, you didn't need a very tall ladder to reach the apples.

Flora Jane Zachary Watkins, who grew up at the Zachary-Tolbert House, wrote in her memoirs regarding the 1860s time period:

> *My father had a nice orchard of apple trees and I have been in the top of every one of them, and gathered some of the most delicious apples anybody ever tasted: Granny Rogers, Morgans and others. Some of the trees are still there or are gone with time.*

Indeed, there are still a few old apple trees growing behind the Zachary-Tolbert House, and as part of the museum's landscape preservation work taking place on the grounds of the historic site, the Cashiers Historical Society and the Cashiers Community Council jointly sponsored "Apple Heritage Day" on March 31 at the Cashiers Community Center. Heritage apple stories were shared, food made with apples was tasted and there was a grafting demonstration and workshop.

John McCarley, a local horticulturalist, will direct the project of identifying and preserving the heritage apple trees at the Zachary-Tolbert House. In the future, you might be able to take a stroll around Mordecai Zachary's restored apple orchard.

WALTER R. TOLBERT, FEDERAL
PROHIBITION AGENT

From the time he was a small boy, Walter Tolbert, son of Robert Red Tolbert and Lucie Collins Tolbert, spent part of his summers at the family's mountain retreat, now known as the Zachary-Tolbert House Museum. In the early 1900s, it was a wonderful treat for the boy and his siblings to escape the heat of South Carolina and explore the natural glories of tiny Cashiers Valley. There, he fished the streams, hiked the nearby mountains and made friends with the local boys who welcomed him into their world.

Walter reached his teen years and matriculated at Bailey Military Institute, a private school located in Greenwood, South Carolina, that was in business from around 1898 until shortly before World War II. He distinguished himself at the institute, excelling at both sports and academics. In his senior year at Bailey, he was named senior caption of the institute, and at a later time, he was an instructor of athletics for the school. He finished his college days at the University of South Carolina.

In the summers, during these teenage years, Walter was quite popular with the girls in Cashiers and would often while away the afternoons playing croquet on the Tolbert's croquet yard in the company of pretty girls. Two of his Cashiers dates were local residents Dana Bird Pell and Madge Dillard, and another girlfriend was Geneva Zachary of Atlanta who spent her summers in Cashiers with her grandparents. They were young, good-looking and brimming with health and the fire of youth. Life was good.

With the advent of the American Prohibition era in 1920, a new federal bureau was created to enforce the generally unpopular amendment. By the

This Augusta, Georgia newspaper headline shows the great sensation caused by the murder of Walter Tolbert and the subsequent electrocution of his killer. *Jane Gibson Nardy.*

mid-1920s, Walter Tolbert had become an experienced federal Prohibition agent. He started his career in Charleston, South Carolina, transferring first to Greenwood, South Carolina, and then in 1927 to Augusta, Georgia, working with county, state and federal officers. He was considered by his peers to be fearless in the discharge of his duties—finding, raiding and destroying stills and bringing the moonshiners to justice. During his year in Augusta, he had become engaged to a local girl and their wedding was planned for July 1928.

On a cold, rainy winter day in February 1928, Walter and two Columbia County, Georgia officers, following tips, had located and destroyed two stills. The trio had placed parts of the stills in their automobile and were headed for the town of Harlem when they suddenly heard firing from a wooded area just off the road. They stopped the car, and as Tolbert rose up to get out of the car, a bullet struck him. He turned to the officers in the car and said, "Boys, they have got me," and then he fell from the running board, face down to the ground, his pistol fully cocked in his right hand, never having been fired. He died on the spot.

In two hours, the biggest manhunt ever staged in that section of Georgia had started, and in a very short time three suspects were in custody and were rushed in automobiles to the Richmond County jail in Augusta. In the meantime, late in the afternoon, George C. Tolbert, one of Walter's brothers, had arrived from Greenwood, South Carolina, to make Walter's funeral arrangements for the following day in Abbeville, South Carolina.

Under intense questioning, suspect Burley Adams, who had already served three terms for violating the National Prohibition Act, confessed that he alone was responsible for the slaying of Tolbert and then revealed the location of the rifle that he had hidden in the hollow of a pine tree. Newspaper reporters were later invited into Adams's jail cell, where he willingly posed for them, holding the murder weapon and smiling. Two trials were held for Burley Adams and in both he was found guilty and sentenced to death in the electric chair.

Three years after the twenty-six-year-old Walter H. Tolbert was laid to rest in Abbeville, South Carolina, his murderer's death sentence was carried out in Georgia. Two days after the electrocution of Burley Adams, his funeral and interment were held at a little Methodist church near the Adams home. Obviously due to morbid curiosity, three thousand people attended the funeral, many bringing elaborate funeral flower arrangements. It is unlikely that Adams, in life, had personally known that many people. His casket was open, and it took over one hour for the mourners to file by for a look—a bizarre ending to just one story of how the thirteen years of Prohibition changed many a life.

THE DR. VAN EPP HOUSE

Each year, the Cashiers Historical Society partners with the Cashiers Area Chamber of Commerce and presents a Village Heritage Award. The call goes out for nominations of an individual or family who has preserved Cashiers's heritage by reusing an older building as a place of business in the community. The structure need not be Historic Register material but can display the creative reuse of one built more recently. The building must contribute to the business vitality of the Cashiers community. The winner is announced at the annual Cashiers Area Chamber of Commerce Banquet in early November, and the Village Heritage Award plaque is presented the following spring.

The 2004 winner was Lyn Monday's House of Design, located one mile from the crossroads on Highway 107 South. The plaque award ceremony will take place at the winning structure, at 7:00 p.m. on Thursday, June 9, 2005, during a chamber of commerce "after hours" celebration. All devotees of preserving our historically significant buildings are invited to attend.

Starting in June 1920, the Dr. Van Epp family of Florida summered in Cashiers Valley. They arrived in a Willys-Overland touring car and boarded the first few years in the Minnie Cole house. In 1923, after the Halsteds of High Hampton died, the Van Epps rented High Hampton and spent two wonderful seasons there until the McKees purchased the estate.

A current-day photo of the Dr. Van Epp house in Cashiers with his granddaughter, Lynn Monday, standing on the front porch. *Jane Gibson Nardy.*

Dr. Van Epp decided he needed his own mountain house, so in 1925, he ordered an Alladin prefabricated home kit from the Alladin Homes catalogue. The company was based in Bay City, Michigan, only one of a number of American companies building prefabricated home kits. Its more famous rivals were Sears, Roebuck and Company and Montgomery Ward. When the kit finally reached Cashiers, it was erected by Joe Wright, a local highly skilled carpenter. The house had four bedrooms, a living and dining room, a kitchen, the first inside bath in the area and front, side and back porches.

Since Dr. Van Epp practiced medicine even while on vacation, the house had outer and inner offices in which to treat patients. There were electric lights from a Delco plant that had to be run two hours daily— most mountain homes would not enjoy electricity until two decades later. The house also had a furnace and fireplaces. There were a large vegetable garden, a cultivated strawberry patch, an asparagus bed and many flower beds and flowering shrubs and fruit trees.

Lynn Monday, the current owner of this house, is a direct descendant of Dr. Van Epp on her mother's side. On Monday's father's side, she is a descendant of the pioneer Norton and Zachary families of Whiteside Cove and Cashiers Valley. She runs a very successful design business from her ancestor's old home.

From the Memory
of Madge Dillard Merrell

SOL'S CREEK SCHOOL
IN LITTLE CANADA

With a starting salary of seventy dollars per month, Madge Dillard, of Cashiers Valley, began her teaching career at Sol's Creek School in Jackson County. The year was 1928, the Great Depression had begun and the area of Little Canada, where Sol's Creek was located, was rather wild and remote. When the day came for Madge to begin her duties at Sol's Creek School, her trunk was securely tied to the top of the family T-Model Ford and she and her father headed north on Highway 107, driving the fifteen-mile trip to Little Canada and to the Merrit Matthews home, where Madge would board for twenty dollars a month. She was feeling homesick even before her father, Tom Dillard, had driven back to Cashiers, but she quickly adjusted to her new life away from home. At the Matthews house, Madge had her own sleeping place on the enclosed porch. Three meals a day were provided and Mrs. Matthews proved to be a good cook. When Madge left for the daily mile walk to school, umbrella in hand in case of rain, she was handed a lunch sack, often containing a sausage biscuit and a piece of pie.

The Matthewses' main occupation was farming, but they also ran a little general store on their property. What Madge remembers most about that store was the candy. Her favorite was the pink, strawberry-flavored marshmallows—six pieces for five cents. The Canada post office was up the road a piece, and Madge often rode the Matthews's horse there

Telling one of her mountain stories to Jane Nardy is Madge Dillard Merrell, on the left. *Jane Gibson Nardy.*

to pick up the mail. Most of Little Canada was known to be of the Republican persuasion, and Mr. Matthews was no exception, going as far as nightly reading aloud from Republican literature. Madge, who was from a staunch Democratic family, asked him to kindly read to himself.

The schoolhouse, also used for church services and a voting precinct, consisted of one main room, a stage, another room beyond the stage and a small cloak room to hang your coat and store your lunch brought from home. There were no bathroom facilities except the woods. The school year lasted only six months, starting in July and closing at Christmas, and Madge was responsible for teaching grades one through seven. The school day began at 8:00 a.m. and lasted until 4:00 p.m., and when the weather was cold, one of the older boys would arrive early and start a fire in the wood stove.

Usually there were twenty to twenty-five students enrolled, and although some of the children were taller than and almost as old as Madge, she encountered no serious discipline problems. Some of the nearly grown boys did ask if they could play kissing games, and although Madge did not agree to that request, she did allow sweethearts to deliver and pick up their notes to each other at the schoolhouse. Outdoors, near the school, the girls had fashioned themselves a playhouse, which was torn up one day by some of the boys, who were actually taken to court in Sylva for their vandalism. Madge had to hire a substitute teacher for a day while she gave testimony in court. Another day, after school, Madge was alone, grading papers in the schoolhouse. Suddenly, she felt the presence of someone behind her and when she looked around, she saw a long rifle barrel pointed at her through the partially opened door. It was a neighbor, Tom Ashe, playing a joke on her.

Madge only spent two nights away from Little Canada during her six-month tenure. The first time she left was to answer the urgent summons of her dying Uncle John Allison in Brevard who longed to see his favorite niece one more time before he died. Unfortunately, when she arrived at the Allison house in Brevard, her uncle had already slipped away.

The second time that Madge spent the night away from Little Canada was for the purpose of voting in her first presidential election. She had only been of voting age for five months and had to return to Cashiers to vote at her home precinct. She was challenged at the polls as to her age, but when her father swore she was twenty-one, she was allowed to cast her ballot. Herbert Hoover was running against Alfred Smith, and Madge voted for Smith. (She has voted in every election in Jackson County since 1928, always true to the Democratic Party.) The next day, back at the Sol's Creek schoolhouse, which had been used the day before for voting, Madge was shocked to find the place in a big mess with papers thrown all around.

Soon it was December, and Madge helped the children put up a Christmas tree, decorated by handmade colorful paper chains. Madge bought each of her students a collapsible cup for a Christmas present so they wouldn't have to drink one after the other from the same dipper. The children seemed to like the cups, but quickly reverted back to the dipper. Thus ended Madge Dillard's first year of teaching.

The History of Jackson County, North Carolina says that Sol's Creek School was abandoned after the spring of 1952. The children in Little Canada began attending the Canada Consolidated School. The Sol's Creek schoolhouse was eventually torn down and the lumber from it was used to build a house.

THE DEATH OF
NORA DEAL

From the remarkable and accurate memory of Madge Dillard Merrell comes this tale of the August 1930 accidental death in Cashiers of eleven-year-old Nora Deal. She was one of the ten children of G. Walker and Cora Picklesimer Deal, all born in South Carolina. Mother Cora was related to the large Cashiers Valley–area pioneer Picklesimer family, a tie that may have accounted for the Deal family moving up into the mountains where they rented the small Ray McCall house. In the 1930 U.S. Population Census of Cashiers Valley Township, Jackson County, we see that Walker Deal was an unemployed sawmill worker, and Madge remembers talk of his weak spot for "John Barleycorn." The oldest son, Raymond Deal, was, at age fifteen, a "water boy" for the State Highway Department, bringing in the only income for a family of twelve. Times were hard for the Deal family, and they would only become harder.

Madge, who had been married less than a month to Merritt, was required in her position as a teacher at the Cashiers school to personally pay a visit to the home of each of her students. The day came when Madge told Nora Deal that she and her husband would be stopping by her house that evening. Very excited, Nora rushed home and told her mother that the teacher was coming by soon. Mrs. Deal told the children to get their "night work" done before the teacher arrived.

From the Memory of Madge Dillard Merrell

Since Cashiers, in 1930, had no electrical power, all household chores were to be completed before dark—thus the expression, "night work."

Gathering enough water to last until the next morning was an important part of the "night work." There was no spring close to the Deal's rented house, but they were allowed to get water from the nearby old Mordecai Zachary spring at the Tolbert's summer home. Carrying empty pails, several of the children, including Nora and her brother, Raymond, with his rifle, started walking to the Zachary spring. Mrs. Deal called out to Raymond, "You be careful around the children with that rifle!" It was as if she had a premonition, for while dipping water from the spring, Raymond's rifle accidentally discharged with a shot that entered Nora's lower abdomen and pierced her intestines seven times. Hearing the screams, the elderly Robert Red Tolbert came to the scene, picked Nora up and carried her back to her home.

It was obvious to all that little Nora was gravely wounded and in need of immediate medical attention. Mr. and Mrs. Lewis, the managers of High Hampton Inn, were summoned, and they arrived with their automobile and offered transportation. Mr. and Mrs. Deal got into the car and they drove to the hospital in Franklin with Mr. Deal holding poor Nora in his lap the whole way. Meanwhile, the remaining nine Deal siblings were taken to the home of Tom and Susan Dillard, Madge's parents, where they were fed and put to bed on pallets laid out on the floor.

At the Zachary spring, located in the woods just behind the Zachary-Tolbert House, pictured here, is where Nora Deal was accidentally shot in the stomach. *Jane Gibson Nardy*.

Dr. Jackson, at the hospital in Franklin, skillfully operated on Nora, but the internal bleeding proved to be too great and she died on the operating table. Mrs. Deal heard the doctor say, "She is gone." The grieving parents gathered up their daughter and got back in the Lewis's car for the long drive back to Cashiers. Walker Deal lovingly held the lifeless body of Nora on the dark return trip and the sad group arrived back in Cashiers at 2:00 a.m. They let their sleeping children remain at the Dillard house but asked Madge to come help with the laying out of the deceased.

Fresh sheets were put on Nora's bed and it was there that Mother Cora and Madge tenderly washed the child's body. Madge clearly remembers trying, in vain, to wash off the stains on Nora's fingers caused by her scraping freshly dug potatoes shortly before her fatal trip to the spring. Next, Nora was dressed, the top sheet was pulled up part way and, finally, a cloth soaked in camphor was placed on her face to deter discoloration.

After daylight, Madge returned home, dressed and went about her teaching duties at the school. At the Deal house, a wooden coffin was soon put together. Nora's body was placed inside, ready for the trip down the mountain to the cemetery in South Carolina. There was no such thing as a florist shop, but Thelma Reid and Maude Fugate fashioned a beautiful cross out of pure white mountain dahlias, placed it atop the casket and Nora Deal left Cashiers on her last earthly journey.

PLEASANT GROVE
SCHOOL IN BULL PEN

In the Jackson County area of Bull Pen stands an old schoolhouse, next to an old cemetery, both named Pleasant Grove. *The History of Jackson County* lists the Pleasant Grove schoolteachers from 1932 until 1940. They were Lucy Monteith, 1932–33; Edith Alley, 1933–34; Hattie Lou Long, 1934–35; Geraldine Shook, 1935–36; and Mrs. Madge D. Merrell, 1937–38 through 1939–40. In the book, *The Cashiers Area—Yesterday, Today and Forever*, there are two pictures of students standing on the steps of Pleasant Grove School in the early 1930s. Besides serving as a schoolhouse, the building was also used as a church, a community meeting place and a voting precinct. The students believed that the school was haunted and said they would hear strange noises inside while everyone was playing outside.

Madge Merrell has shared her memories of the years she lived in Bull Pen while teaching at Pleasant Grove. She and her husband, Merritt, with their two little boys, Dink and Curtis, first lived in the Lawton McCall house near the old "Wrack" McCall Mill. Mica mining was being conducted nearby. On more than one occasion, while she and her husband lay sleeping, a snake or salamander crawled across their faces. Often, while living at the McCall house, Catherine McCall would come for the day to baby-sit, cook, wash and iron the clothes. She charged three dollars per week.

The Pleasant Grove School and church building is where Madge Dillard Merrell taught the children of the Bull Pen area. *Jane Gibson Nardy.*

The Merrell's second residence in Bull Pen was in an unfinished house that belonged to Cecil White. There were cracks in the walls through which the wind would blow, making it a cold place to live in the winter.

The Merrells' third home was located right beside Bull Pen Road. It was a Sears and Roebuck tent that was tightly secured to a wooden platform. There was also a small kitchen by the side of the tent. Madge cooked on a "step stove," which consisted of an oven with room on top for two pots. To warm the tent, there was a stove made from thin tin that put out abundant heat. Birch wood was used for fuel and it produced a wonderful aroma. Husband Merritt built the family an outhouse at an acceptable distance from the tent. A good flowing spring was located not far away. For two years, the Merrells lived in the tent and Madge remembers it as being quite comfortable—especially warm and cozy in the winters.

One day, a strange man stopped by the tent home and told Madge that he wanted to buy some bootleg whiskey. Madge, feeling highly insulted to be asked such a question, gave the man a lecture.

I want you to know that I'm a lady and a schoolteacher. I live here with my husband and two little boys. We have nothing to do with selling whiskey and don't you ever stop here again.

He quickly left and never returned.

From the Memory of Madge Dillard Merrell

Occasionally, Madge's parents, Tom and Susan Dillard, would come get their grandson, Curtis, Madge's youngest child, and take him to stay with them for a while in Cashiers. On one such visit, Curtis slipped, fell from the front porch and broke his leg. The Dillards rushed him down to Brevard, where doctors at the Shriner's Hospital set the little fellow's leg.

It was about a mile from the tent to the school and each day Madge, along with her eldest son, Dink, walked that mile to reach the schoolhouse. The school day lasted from 8:30 in the morning until 4:00 in the afternoon, and the school year only lasted for about six months. Pleasant Grove School even had an outhouse—an improvement over the sanitary arrangements at Little Canada's Sol's Creek School, where she had previously taught.

The number of students varied from only seven to a maximum of twenty. There were McCall and Rochester and Rice children, but Madge most clearly remembers the Lusk children with their innovative given names. There were the Lusk siblings: Sexton, his twin, Dexton, and their brother, Lexton. Another Lusk family had children Whelosia, Sota, Zula, Zuland, Zeland, Nita and Mita.

Many of the women Madge knew in Bull Pen were engaged in weaving on the old-fashioned looms. They specialized in coverlets but also wove linsey wool for dresses. Poke berries and white and black walnuts were some of the natural ingredients used for dying the thread. Sisters Ida McCall and Teag McCall were well known for their weaving. Many people raised sheep in the Bull Pen area, and after the sheep had grown a thick coat, there would be a sheep-shearing day, followed by washing the wool and laying it on white sheets out in the sun to dry. Next, the thread was made by placing the wool in rows on a "card." There is a picture of Aunt Teag McCall standing by her spinning wheel in the book, *The Cashiers Area, Yesterday, Today and Forever.*

The old Pleasant Grove School building still stands today and is in active use by the Pleasant Grove Baptist Church congregation. To the left of and slightly behind the building is a long, covered shed with picnic tables for spreading out the food for dinner on the grounds or at family reunions. To the right of the building is the Pleasant Grove Cemetery with the tombstones carved with the names of many early area residents. Some of the graves are still "mounded," and a few are made of soapstone, in the fashion of yesteryear.

WILLIAM NORTON'S DAUGHTERS AND THE BUSHWHACKERS

From April 1861 through the spring of 1865, the Civil War exacted a heavy toll on the citizens of Cashiers Valley. The first part of the war saw sons, husbands and fathers joining the Confederacy and marching away to an unknown fate, while other families held fast to their strong Union sentiments. The last couple of years of the war brought real physical suffering to the area. While there were no major battles fought here, there were the casualties of divided family loyalties, bushwhacker raids and near starvation.

Greene County Tennessee's Union officer, Colonel George Washington Kirk, led a band of "legal" bushwhackers who, many times, rode into the valley spreading fear and rode out of the valley with confiscated livestock and provisions. Known locally as "Kirk's Army" or "Kirk's Raiders," this group of men, under orders, had to find their own food, and all homes in their path were ransacked for flour, sugar and meat. The local people quickly learned clever means of concealing their food. Some civilians took their hams out into a rocky field and covered them with moss so they looked like boulders. Another hiding place was the nearby creek, where bags of flour were submerged and covered with rocks. It seems the flour would harden around the edges but the middle would stay dry.

The raiders always carried a branding iron with them and if they were lucky enough to discover an able-bodied horse, they would take the branding iron into a house, stick it into the fireplace until it was red hot and then go back outside and brand the stolen horse with "U.S. Army."

The William Norton–Susannah Zachary Norton home, which contained at least eight children, was visited at least twice by the bushwhackers. William Norton, one of the sons of Whiteside Cove founder Barak Norton, had built his house near the center of Cashiers Valley, along the road that came up from South Carolina. Soyrieta Vap Epp, in her book *Status Quo*, gave a description of the house in earlier days:

> *It is two-story, of notched, grooved and pegged construction, puncheon floors and hand riveted cedar shingles. Originally it had enormous stone fireplaces chinked with clay, as were the pine logs. The windows were small and shuttered, parchment covered the openings; they could not afford glass. A long covered dog trot led to the separate kitchen. The massive native stone fireplace stretched across the entire west wall and had a raised hearth and iron cranes that swung out, fitted with hooks on which pots and kettles could be hung. Iron pots, pans and footed Dutch ovens hung nearby.*

According to Van Epp, the William Norton house was remodeled in 1946. The outbuildings, dog trot and detached kitchen were torn down, but the house remains standing and is in use today. There is a mail slot still visible from the days that William Norton was the postmaster of Cashiers.

Prior to the first bushwhacker visit, William and Susannah Norton had carefully hidden their supply of cured meat inside the house behind the wall paneling. They instructed their children to never tell anyone, especially the bushwhackers, that the family had any meat. Well, one day, Kirk's Raiders rode up to the Norton's house, dismounted, went inside and demanded that the family give them any meat they had. They were told there was no meat to turn over. Suddenly, one of the younger Norton daughters looked at her parents and said, "Don't you remember, you hid it behind the wall boards?"

On the second visit the Nortons had from Colonel George W. Kirk and his men, there was a new demand. Kirk looked William Norton straight in the eye and said,

> *My men would like to have a square dance this evening and we need some young ladies to be our partners. If you will allow your daughters to come with us, we will treat them like ladies and we will return them safely and unharmed to you. If you won't let them come with us, we'll burn your house down.*

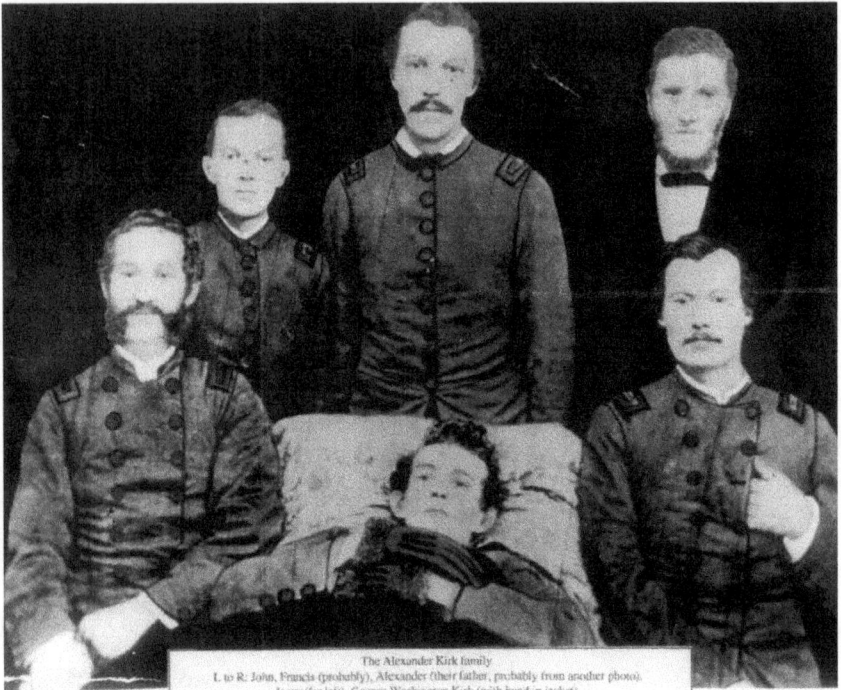

The Alexander Kirk family
L. to R: John, Francis (probably), Alexander (their father, probably from another photo).
James (far left), George Washington Kirk (with hand in jacket).
The reclining brother is William, wounded at Knoxville in 1864.

Greene County, Tennessee's Kirk family is pictured here in Union Civil War uniforms, with Colonel George Washington Kirk sitting at front right. *Jane Gibson Nardy.*

Off went Mary Arlissa, age twenty; Elizabeth Alice, age sixteen; and Julia M., around age thirteen. The oldest sister, Sarah Emmalissa, age twenty-two, was married, but her husband was likely away and she may have attended the dance. The youngest sister, Martha Lou Ellen Norton, was only about age eleven, so she would have remained at home.

True to their word, a few anxious hours later, the bushwhackers returned the Norton daughters to their home in the same condition they had been in when they left. Of all the many stories told about the feared bushwhackers, this is the only one with a happy ending.

Selected Zachary Stories

CASHIERS VALLEY
IN 1877

In the spring of 1877 in Cashiers Valley, Alexander Zachary, age seventy, took pen in hand and wrote to his youngest son, Thompson Roberts Zachary, who had established a homestead in faraway Kansas. There was news from Cashiers Valley as well as questions about the welfare of T.R. and several of his siblings also living in the West.

Cashiers Valley
April 12th, 1877
Dear son:

I received your card dated March 19th which found us all in common health and doing very well. We have plenty here to live upon as yet and I think will. I am glad to think you are doing so well in your country. Hope you may continue doing so. I have not got entirely well of the erysipelas yet. I have it in my blood and it is hard to get out. It hurts me in my feet worst, still there is no sign outwardly, they have a burning sensation which pesters me a little at times.

The rest are all well. Of course you want to know how the people in this country is doing. I have just been out to James [Alexander's son, James Madison Zachary] *at Grassey Camp* [Norton], *he has just got one of the best saw mills to running I ever saw. I suppose it will cut 2000 feet every day, he will soon have the road done to it. The mill is east of D. Norton's on Grassey Camp Creek. A.W.* [Alexander's son, Alexander Washington Zachary, called "Wash"] *is getting on all right, a man from Charleston, S.C. is building near him—just across the Blue Ridge towards the Jenney cabin fronting Whiteside. I have not had a letter for sometime from C.C.* [Alexander's eldest son, Christopher Columbus Zachary] *therefore I cannot say how he is doing, but I suppose very well. It seems he has not time to write or don't care. I want to hear from all my children often that has left me and gone west. Is C.C. making money fast herding cattle or not? I would like to know how he came out with his cattle last fall, how many did he sell and how many did he keep through the winter, and what kind of winter you have had.*

We had here the prettiest March you ever saw with the exception of the last day or two. Your mother and I was then in Walhalla. At that time we was badly pestered to get home. We came up through the Cove for the best way, was 7 days on the road. Coming down the mountain we run up upon a sheet of ice about 30 yards wide and [it appears a sentence is missing here]...*very sidelong, brought it over by hand, run off the lower side, of course, luckily got help at once, got back, came on then all right to the shed. Going up from the river got help and came on to the next and so on until we got home.*

A snow scene on one of the old roads in Cashiers, reminiscent of the weather described in Alexander Zachary's 1877 letter. *Jane Gibson Nardy.*

We are at this time having big frosts every night. This month has been colder than last. We are having cold nights and warm days. I think most of our fruit has gone up, still there are some peaches yet. We have two stores in the Valley. Your Uncle Jonathan and a man by the name of Cline has them.

You wish to know all about our ancestors—I am not prepared at this time to tell you much about them. Your Great-Grandfather was named William, had four sons, John, David, William, James. The old man came from England, was a brick mason by trade; built a large brick building on a good farm and lived there until his death, never moving. He had two daughters, Mary and Elizabeth. Mary married a man by the name of Todd and Elizabeth Jack Garges. Both went west, you know some of them. Uncle Joshuary Roberts moved west about 65 years since—there are a great many of them somewhere. John was drowned in the Ohio River, never married. Wm. Lived in Virginia, also Stone Boyd and Douglas, marrying my mother's sisters. Some of the rest of them lived and died in Surry, N.C. on Stewart's Creek, the wealthiest part of the county. I don't suppose Uncle Jonathan's land could be bought today for 50,000, lying on Stewart's Creek.

I only mentioned A.W. and J.M. The rest of them are doing very well. George Cole and Manda [Alexander's daughter Amanda] *is living with us. Between us we have 23 head of cattle, plenty to make our milk and beef.*
Your affectionate father,
Alex. Zachary

UNCLE ROY'S 1920 AND 1921
CHRISTMAS LETTERS

B etween 1910 and 1920, Bird Zachary of Cashiers married Ernest
Raines of Lake Toxaway and they soon ventured to Washington
State, accompanied by Bird's brother, Roy Zachary, and his small
daughter, Flora. Roy's wife, Christina Louise Quy, had died in
Cashiers on December 4, 1917, a few years after the birth of Flora.
Like many other young adult mountain men in and around Cashiers,
Ernest Raines and Roy Zachary easily found work with the lumber
business in the Cascade Mountains of Washington. They settled in the
town of Snoqualmie Falls, located at a high altitude where there were
bountiful snows all winter.

The eldest brother of Bird Zachary Raines and Roy Zachary was John
A. Zachary, who had lived in Atlanta, Georgia, since about 1900 where
he first made his living teaching school and then became an employee
of the railroad mail service. He had married Viola Crossley of Monroe,
Georgia, in 1904, and they became the parents of Geneva Zachary in
1906 and Julia Luckie Zachary in 1910, both born in Atlanta. Sadly, John
died in 1919 of tuberculosis from which he had suffered for years. His
widow and his young daughters struggled to make ends meet.

Just prior to Christmas 1920, when John A. Zachary had been dead for
a year, his brother in Washington State wrote the following letter to John's
children in Atlanta:

Roy Zachary climbing Mount Pisgah near Brevard, North Carolina, with niece, Jane Gibson, on his shoulders. Circa 1939. *Jane Gibson Nardy.*

Snoqualmie Falls, Wash.
Dec. 17, 1920
Dear Geneva, Julia and [your] *Mother:*

As the time draws near, I can't help but think of how John used to plan a Merry Christmas for others. It is more than likely that you will miss him more at Christmas time than on any other occasion.

I am sending check for $10.00 which is intended to buy a little something for each of you. May you be reminded that others think of you even tho the one who meant so much to you has gone. It is not wise to buy presents out here to send back East. Everything is so much more expensive out here. So you may select your own presents. No doubt you will be better suited than if I made the selection.

We are all well and Ernest and I are still working altho the big mill has ceased operation. Things look pretty close out here. There are thousands of people out of employment in the cities.

I must close now and write home [Meaning Cashiers Valley]. *Am trying not to forget any of those who might be expecting something from me this Christmas. This is the first Christmas that has found me out of debt since 1908.*

Love to you all. Would like to hear from each of you when you feel like writing.
From your Uncle Roy.

The following year, in December 1921, Uncle Roy wrote a very similar letter to Geneva and Julia Zachary with a check enclosed for Christmas. He added:

Your Aunt Bird and I often talk of how we would like to have you girls pay us a visit sometime and we will continue to hope to see you someday. I expect to be married next week to a girl who was born and raised in Sweden. She is 24 years old and has only been in America six years. She speaks English without any accent and most people who know her can't understand how she could have learned to speak English so well in such a short time.

This letter ended:

I think of you often and can understand what a comfort you are to your mother who is left to fight alone the battle. Love to Mother and girls from your Uncle Roy. December 14, 1921.

CASHIERS GHOST BUSTER

There is a ghost story that has been told around Cashiers for over half a century that tells about Louisa Emmalie Zachary Heaton (1846–97) who committed suicide, turned herself into a white owl and now haunts the guests at High Hampton Inn. This frightening tale has appeared several times in print, including the book *Mountain Ghost Stories and Curious Tales of Western North Carolina*. The four-page short story "Hannibal Heaton Hears a Hoot" has a little bit of truth in it—Emmalie did kill herself, and her husband, Hannibal Heaton, had sold her land against her wishes—but research now proves that most of the story is incorrect.

Let us take a look at what has been repeated so many times compared to the actual facts as found in deeds, federal censuses, Georgia cemetery records, interviews with family members, photographs and newspaper records:

1. General Wade Hampton built High Hampton Inn in 1850.
The truth: Wade Hampton did not purchase land in Cashiers until 1855.
2. Emmalie told Hannibal that if he sold the land she would hang herself from the tree out front.
The truth: She hanged herself in the stable.
3. Emmalie's hair had turned pure white when she was in her twenties.
The truth: Pictures of her show that she had dark hair until her death.
4. When Hannibal climbed the tree to cut his wife down, a large white

A sixteen-year-old Emmaline Leona Zachary Moody, in 1862, poses for a picture to send to her soldier husband who was in the Union army. *Barbara Chambless.*

Ethel Averreller Heaton, one of the daughters of Hannibal Heaton and Emmaline Zachary Moody Heaton. Photo taken in 1929. *Barbara Chambless.*

owl, the same color as his wife's hair, attacked him, forcing him to retreat. Neighbors came to his aid.

The truth: Emmalie was hanging in the stable and her hair was not white.

5. Within a week of Emmalie's burial, Hannibal Heaton had disappeared and was never heard from again.

The truth: According to the 1900 federal census of Macon County, North Carolina, Hannibal Heaton had moved to the little community of Ellijay, North Carolina, between Highlands and Franklin. By 1901, he had moved to White County, Georgia, where he died and was buried in 1902.

Sylva's weekly newspaper, the *Sylva Sentinel*, carried the following article in its next issue after Emmalie's demise:

> *Mrs. Heaton, wife of Hannibal Heaton of Cashiers Valley Township in this county, committed suicide by hanging herself with a rope in the stable last Sunday afternoon. When her husband learned the fact, he attempted to destroy his life by cutting two fearful gashes in his throat when he was prevented from doing further injury to himself.*

Many years before her suicide, Emmalie had told her cousin, Tom Dillard, that after she died she would still be seen walking around the valley. She also predicted that when she died, black dogs would fight over her body. Sure enough, swore Tom Dillard, when they cut her down, there were black dogs fighting nearby. And when you're driving down NC 107 South at night, around the entrance to High Hampton Inn, please slow down. Black dogs are known to fight in that area.

This story is only a small part of the jinxed life of Emmalie Zachary Heaton. If you ever hear the full story, you'll have no doubt that truth can be much stranger than fiction.

BIRD ZACHARY RAINES AND THE BOX TURTLE

S tarting in the early 1980s and continuing for over twenty years, Alberta Jenkins Zachary wrote a weekly column for the Cashiers newspaper, *Crossroads Chronicle*. The "Country Kitchen" always contained at least one recipe, but what makes these articles so valuable are the bits of early Cashiers Valley history Alberta wove in around the food talk. She drew upon her own personal experiences, as well as those of her husband, her mother-in-law and her many contemporaries, giving her readers glimpses of mountain living back into the nineteenth century.

In one of her columns, the exact date is unknown, she wrote about the eastern box turtle, found in abundance in these Western North Carolina mountains.

> *I have always thought the first sighting of the* [box] *turtle as a sign of spring as dependable as the arrival of the first cat bird. About 40 years ago,* [1940s?] *I found an unusually large turtle here on our place* [the old T.R. Zachary homestead in Cashiers]. *I turned it over and plainly carved on the under shell was "M.B.Z.—May 10th, 1900."*
>
> *I told my sister-in-law, Bird Raines, about this. She said her brother, John Zachary, had carved his initials, those of his four siblings and the date of the carving on turtle shells. The initials M.B.Z. were*

From left to right, Willie Thomas Zachary, Bird Zachary Raines and Ruth Zachary, all sisters-in-law. *Jane Gibson Nardy.*

hers—"*Maggie Bird Zachary,*" and she was 16 years old at the time. [Since Bird was born in January of 1886, she would have actually been age 14 in 1900.]

We took the venerable turtle to the Shell Station—the one that until recently was at the intersection. A man picked it up to examine it. It bit him and he dropped it. We let it go. Ten or twelve years later, we found it again—right here on our place! I wonder how long it took for him to creep back up here? Several years later we found it a third time and showed it to several people and took a picture of it—not a very good one. I still have it somewhere.

Checking a few sites on the Internet, we learn that box turtles go into hibernation in the late fall. They burrow as far as two feet deep into loose earth, mud, stream bottoms, old stump holes or mammal burrows. They usually emerge from hibernation in April. They have a home range of 750 feet or less in which they normally stay, and they may live as long as a hundred years.

When she was widowed in the 1950s, Bird Zachary Raines had returned to Cashiers after living about forty years in Washington State and California. Her only daughter became a movie star, but therein lies another story. She built a little cottage down the hill from her brother and sister-in-law, Howard and Alberta Zachary, who themselves lived at the old place where Bird had been born. Bird was so happy to be home for good, and she looked forward to living out her life surrounded by family and childhood memories. That proved to be a short time, as cancer came calling and she died in early January 1957.

Jon Zachary, son of the late Howard and Alberta Zachary, is presently living at the old place. He remembers as a youngster seeing the box turtle a few times, and when he would pick it up, it wouldn't even retract its head back into its shell. Jon was eight or ten years old the summer after Bird Zachary Raines was buried in the Upper Zachary Cemetery. Her retirement cottage was unoccupied, as her estate had not been completely settled. A few months after her funeral, someone was hired to cut the little plot of grass beside Bird's house and the lawn mower accidentally ran over the box turtle, ending its life in middle age. Ironic, isn't it, that Bird and her namesake box turtle each met their demise in the same year?

OCTOBER 1878 LETTER FROM T.R. ZACHARY TO HIS FIANCÉE IN GEORGIA

Thompson Roberts "T.R." Zachary, who was born in Cashiers Valley in 1850, temporarily moved west in the late 1860s, living first with his older brother Christopher Columbus Zachary in Missouri and then striking out on his own, homesteading in Rush County, Kansas. By 1878, when he penned the following letter, he was engaged to be married to Julia Beazley of Union Point, Georgia.

> *October 6, 1878, Rush County, Kansas, postmarked Great Bend, Kansas, addressed to Miss Julia L. Beazley, Union Point, Greene County, Georgia.*
>
> *Olney, Rush County, Kansas*
>
> *My dear Julia,*
>
> *After some delay I will endeavor to interest you for a little while at least, but I fear my efforts will only be an attempt. I received your kind letter over a week ago and would have written last Sunday had you not made the request of me to write today. I am glad, however, that you made this request for now I will have the pleasure of reading two letters from you to the one from me, do you see? Unless you insist that we get up a kind of a double correspondence which would, I think in the end, might cause a collision. I mean the letters would be apt to "collide" as*

Thompson Roberts Zachary and his first wife, Julia L.M. Beazley Zachary, who met while he was selling seeds/fruit trees to farmers in Georgia. *Jane Gibson Nardy.*

our mailing facilities are not as such as would enable us to write with the necessary regularity. I suppose, according to your proposition that you are writing to me today Friday, at this very moment. (tis now about ten o'clock) What a pleasure it would be for me to know just what you were writing. Then I would be able to surprise my little "Tret" by answering her questions in advance. If only I could see you this morning it would differ but little what you were writing about, and Julia, if God spares my life, a pleasure <u>similar</u> shall be ours in the future. There is a pleasure even in the thought that our weary separation will come to an end. Say, Julia, save those kisses until I come there and you will have something <u>real</u> to kiss. God bless you, even the thought makes me happy to think you love me so much as to kiss my signature. I honestly believe that in you I will find a noble and loving wife, one whose affections will never grow dim. God forbid that they should, for then I should consider that <u>my</u> happiness was at an everlasting end. Is it possible for man and wife to live happily together? If so, then I have no fears but what true happiness will be ours. I have a forgiving disposition and feel confident through the expressions set forth in your letter that now lies before me, that it is possible for us to live a happy life. I shall ever be ready to forgive you and to over look your faults (if any). I know there are very few people who are faultless. I am sure I have many and really hope you will point them out before they become offensive to you. I consider you doing me a cruel injustice if you were to discover some fault in me that was the least annoying to you and not tell me of the same. This, I think, is the cause of so much unpleasant feelings that spring up between married persons. I will send you a piece of poetry that will somewhat express my views on the subject. 'Tis as you say, we know nothing of each others characters. So far as my character is concerned, think it is as good or a little better than those of the average young man. I am saying this *myself*, nevertheless I believe it to be the fact.

I have always made it a point to act the gentleman wherever I have gone, have always courted friendship with everyone and today I can say that I only have one enemy. There is not one place in all my travels where I have become acquainted that I would not be welcomely received. This much goes for "self praise." Enough of that—wish I could think of something to write that I know would be pleasant for you to read. Believe I will only write four pages this time, then Friday I will get to hear you *scold* a little.

Well, I am fixing up for winter and will begin my house next week. I think I have a very nice home site. Last spring I set out a row of cottonwood all around, making a square of 70 by 100 yards. They are growing beautifully. This fall I will plant a row of trees round five acres north of the house for an orchard, garden, etc.

I am as lonesome as a cat today. Hope I will get a letter written by the best girl in Georgia today. I will try to answer your letter of today before I hear from this one as there is not much in this to hear from. I remain your devoted lover, T.R.

(You say there is a great many things you would like to tell me, but think best to wait until you see me. Now, Julia, please don't *do* me this way, tell me everything and rest assured that I will respect you for doing do.)

A MOTHER'S LAMENT

Within a year after the death of a Cashiers Valley teenager, her mother, Elizabeth Zachary Allison, daughter of Colonel John A. Zachary, wrote a sixteen-page memorial about her daughter's last year. This impressive manuscript came to light a few years ago when Ben Zachary of Brevard, North Carolina, turned over to me a brown paper bag of Zachary family papers, which had been handed down in his family for over a hundred years. Following are some excerpts from that tribute to Mellie Allison from her grieving mother. It is dated 1870.

Margaret M. Allison, daughter of Elizabeth and E.L. Allison was born March the 9th 1850 and died 20 minutes past 7 o'clock p.m. on the 7th of April 1869, aged 19 years and 28 days. Mellie, as we called her from her earliest childhood, was remarkably kind and affectionate. She joined the Church at about the age of nine years. Then when stern disease came and prostrated her delicate frame, she never uttered one murmur. Previous to her death she was confined for three months and ten days and suffered such throes of pain.

Although she was anxious to get well until a few days before her death, she left nothing relating either to earth or heaven undone. She dispersed of her little store of earthly goods with composure. She told me to plant roses and flowers around her grave and said she'd always expected to plant them around my grave. She said there was no need for her to take anymore medicine as it could do her no good.

On Sunday, the 4th of April she was fast fading away from the paths of earth. We took her to hear the Rev. Edwards preach and she lay quiet listening to the sermon. When it ended she asked that all in the church come speak to her as she seemed to know it would be the last opportunity some of them would have this side of the grave. She would often beg us to wash her face to keep her alive until her sister could get there. In a few days her sister arrived and Mellie smiled and said, "Sarah Ann, they all thought I would die before you could get here."

On Monday morning she hurried her friends to make her dress she was to be buried in. After it was done, she asked her sister to try it on so she might see if it would fit her. She examined it as carefully as if it had been her wedding dress. She invited some friends to come back when she died and help robe her for the grave. Her last evening alive she was carried outside so she could once more behold her surroundings and see the spring with the laurels surrounding it and the nearby peach trees filled with buds.

Returning to the house, Mellie lay calm and quiet, folding her hands across her breast. She passed away as faintly as the passing of a summer breeze or an evening cloud, and without a single groan, she sweetly fell asleep and our beloved Mellie was no more.

If some of you reading this have a rose and a few minutes to spare one day, why don't you stop by the Lower Zachary Cemetery in Cashiers and put that rose on Mellie's grave?

The lower Zachary Cemetery grave of Margaret M. "Mellie" Allison, a much-loved teenaged daughter of Elizabeth Zachary Allison and E. Logan Allison. *Jane Gibson Nardy.*

THE ACE AND THE ACTRESS

B rigadier General Robin Olds, air force fighter pilot extraordinaire, died at his home in Steamboat Springs, Colorado, on June 14, 2007. After his graduation from the U.S. Military Academy at West Point in 1943, he quickly earned his wings as a fighter pilot in World War II, becoming a double ace before the end of that war.

Robin had ties to Cashiers, a place he had visited many times, that began with his Hollywood marriage in 1947 to movie star Ella Wallace Raines, whose mother, Bird Zachary, was born in Cashiers Valley in 1886. Ella's father was Ernest Raines, who was from the large Raines family of the Lake Toxaway area. He was one of the North Carolina mountain men with experience in logging who moved to Washington State early in the 1900s to log the beautiful western mountains. In the year of 1920 at Snoqualmie Falls, Washington, Bird gave birth to Ella, an only child, much doted on by both parents. Ella's father turned her into an excellent horsewoman, a confident skier and an expert sharpshooter, while her mother taught Ella gourmet cooking skills and clothing design.

In 1947, both Ella and Robin were in the midst of busy, high profile, exotic careers. Hollywood was giving Ella the "star treatment" with almost daily appearances at events covered by photographers and gossip columnists—not to mention the movies she was making both on the lot in Hollywood or off on some distant location. Prior to marrying Robin, Ella had appeared in at least ten movies. Even when she had a small part, she

Ella Wallace Raines and her second husband, General Robin Olds, enjoying one of their favorite sports. They were a good-looking couple. *Jane Gibson Nardy.*

was always the female lead. In her 1944 movie *Tall in the Saddle*, with John Wayne, she is remembered for her scenes on horseback and for throwing a knife at John Wayne that narrowly missed him. She had four movies released the year she and Robin married.

Robin's life was just as hectic as his wife's. The U.S. Air Force was officially formed in 1947—he joined the country's first military jet squadron and was wingman on the air force's first jet aerobatic team, and he was the first foreigner to command an elite fighter unit of Britain's Royal Air Force. He was well liked by the troops, but because of his maverick ways, he was denied combat duty in the Korean Conflict. He made up for that by an outstanding performance in Vietnam, where he became a triple ace. In 259 missions in two wars, Robin was never shot down or wounded.

During their almost thirty-year marriage, Robin was stationed at many locations, both in the United States and in other countries, and Ella would often join him with their two daughters. After Vietnam, General Olds spent three years as a popular commandant of the Air Force Academy in Colorado Springs, where Ella was known for her entertaining. The ace and the actress divorced in 1975, with a comment from Ella that it was impossible to live with a warrior who had no war. She died near Los Angeles in 1988. During his retirement, Robin gave lectures, worked on an autobiography, skied and, less than a year before his death, appeared as a commentator on the History Channel's series *Dogfights*, describing his action in Vietnam and his air battles in World War II.

THE BALLAD OF
KIDDER COLE

My name is Felix Eugene Alley
My best gal lives in Cashiers Valley;
She's the joy of my soul
And her name is Kidder Cole

I don't know—it must have been by chance,
'Way last fall when I went to a dance,
I was to dance with Kidder Cole the livelong night
But got my time beat by Charley Wright

These are the first two of the fifteen stanzas of "The Ballad of Kidder Cole," written over a hundred years ago by a heartsick teenage boy from Whiteside Cove. His arch rival and cousin, Charley/Charlie Wright, resided in Highlands, and the object of their affection, Olive Kidder Cole, was the local beauty in Cashiers Valley. Many of you reading this article will recognize the name of Charlie Wright, as he gained nationwide recognition for his bravery in 1911 when he rescued a friend who had fallen from Whiteside Mountain. This past July's "Walk in the Park" featured his wife, Helen Wright Wilson, who built Helen's Barn for square dancing a few years after Charlie died. But how many of you have heard the names of Felix Eugene Alley and Kidder Cole?

On Thursday, September 15, 2005, the Cashiers Historical Society conducted a ramble based on the old ballad's three characters. A visit was first made to Lombard's Lodge in Whiteside Cove, where Felix Eugene Alley was born on July 5, 1873, the son of Colonel John H. Alley and Sarah Whiteside Norton. Howard Eugene Alley, author of *Presumed Dead, A Civil War Mystery*, and an Alley family descendant, told the life story of Felix, who became a popular judge in Western North Carolina as well as an author. To hear the story, the ramble group stood in front of the actual house where Felix Alley was born.

Moving on to Cashiers Valley, a visit was made to the house where Kidder Cole, the daughter of Sheriff George M. Cole and Sarah Amanda "Mandy" Zachary, was born on October 14, 1878. There, at the old house known locally as the Cole-Tate House, Diane Phillips, a direct descendant of Kidder Cole, entertained all with the fascinating life story of Kidder Cole. Diane, who lives in Hendersonville, shared a large portfolio of Cole photographs, portraits and memorabilia.

In the 1880 U.S. Population Census of Jackson County, North Carolina, we find George M. Cole, occupation "merchant," and Mandy Cole, his wife, living in Cashiers Valley with their first two children, Frank W. and Olive Kidder. Later, two other daughters, Rosa and Gracie, were added to complete the family. In the 1890s, the decade of Kidder Cole's fame, besides enjoying the attention of many young men, Kidder attended a Female Academy in Anderson, South Carolina, boarding there with her mother's sister, Aunt Ellen Zachary Coffee. Also, in this time period, George M. Cole continued running his general store, which was attached to the main house and was where the earliest telephone in the valley was located. At this same location, Cole served as the postmaster of Cashiers Valley for a number of years. Just before the end of the 1890s, Kidder Cole got married—not to Felix Eugene Alley nor Charlie Wright, but to a physician named "Little Doc" Nichols.

Finally, the group carpooled to Highlands and visited the site of the January 17, 1873 birth of Charles Nicholas Wright. The actual house no longer stands. He was the son of Barak Wright and Virginia Green and the grandson of James Wright and Jemima Norton. Gathered at the home of Linda Wright David and Kenton David, a recording of "The Ballad of Kidder Cole" was played. Then, Maxie Wright Duke, the youngest child of Charlie Wright, told her father's life story. Charlie Wright was not only immortalized in Felix Alley's poem, but he became a real life hero. A book, titled *Courage at Fool's Rock, A True Tale of Incredible Heroism at Whiteside*

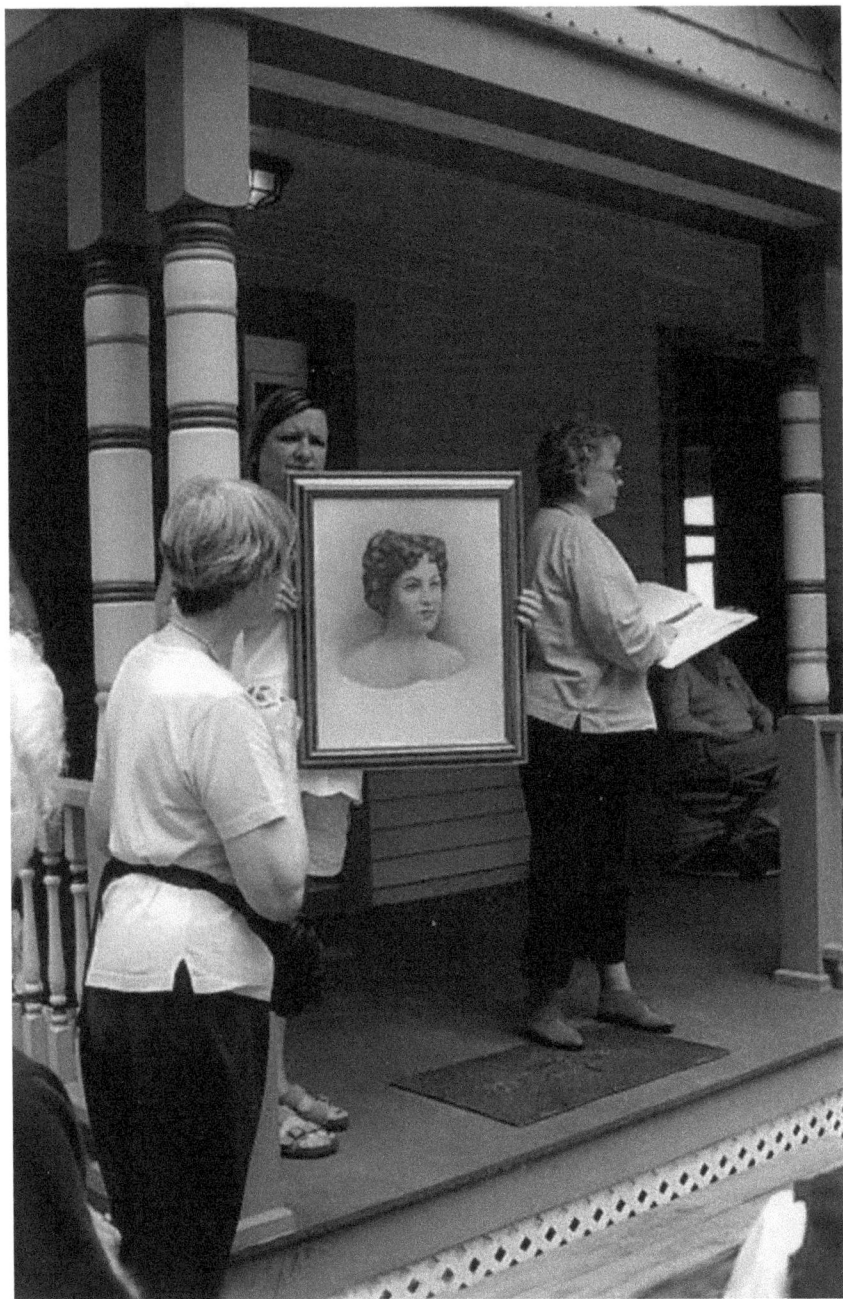

A portrait of Olive Kidder Cole, held up by Liz Nardy Millis at the Cole-Tate House during a Cashiers Historical Society "Ramble." *Gay Kattel.*

Mountain, was written by Bill Marett and published in 1975, and it details how Charlie Wright saved the life of Gus Baty. During a May 1911 picnic on top of Whiteside Mountain, Gus fell off the mountain, and for hours he was left precariously dangling, holding onto a small bush. Charlie successfully crawled down the mountainside and helped Gus back up to the top. The incident was investigated by the Andrew Carnegie Hero Award Commission, which led to Charlie Wright being presented a gold medal. He was also given a cash award of $2,000. The solid gold medal still remains in the hands of Charlie Wright's descendants.

Neither Felix Eugene Alley nor Charlie Wright won the hand of Kidder Cole in marriage, but all lived interesting lives. Felix became a well-known Western North Carolina politician; Charlie Wright became a hero; and Kidder Cole kept her fame as a beauty.

STORY OF THE
ZACHARY CLOCK

This is the story of a rare, nineteenth-century grandfather clock, made
by Silas Hoadley of Connecticut, and brought from Surry County,
North Carolina, to Cashiers Valley by the pioneer Zachary family in the early
1830s. Colonel John Alexander Zachary, his wife Sarah Roberts Zachary and
thirteen of their fourteen children traveled to their new home on a perilous
journey, as later related by one of the daughters, Elizabeth Zachary Allison.
One night, during the trip, a big storm came up, with a strike of lightning
splitting and toppling a tree directly onto the wagon where the family's prize
clock had been carefully placed. The tree narrowly missed the clock.

Elizabeth remembered the long, tiresome move—their belongings
packed in a six-horse wagon with Mrs. Zachary and the youngest children
following in a carriage. They made their way southwest, dipping briefly
into South Carolina and then turning north and parallel to follow the
crude Native American trail that meandered beside the Chattooga
River—up, up, until they reached their destination at the headwaters of
the Chattooga. They probably paused in Whiteside Cove to speak with
their new neighbors, the Norton family.

Until 1819, this land was part of the Cherokee Nation. After the "Love
Survey" of 1820, the State of North Carolina opened the area to settlers.
Grants of 640 acres were available for a pittance, but few pioneers

The face of Colonel John Alexander Zachary's grandfather clock made by Silas Hoadley of Connecticut in the early 1800s. *Jane Gibson Nardy.*

chose to claim land in the rugged area just north of South Carolina and Georgia, and only the hardiest ventured into that wilderness. Colonel Zachary and several of his grown sons applied for land in what would become Cashiers Valley—land that until 1851 lay in Macon County.

Land was cleared, sturdy houses were built and in the living room of the colonel's home stood the grandfather clock, tall and stately, keeping time over the years with its unusual wooden clock movements.

According to most modern-day Zachary family descendants, the story ended with the safe journey of the clock, but in the last few years, the rest of the clock story has been revealed. When Colonel Zachary died in 1872, he left the clock and his personal papers to his eldest son, Alfred Zachary. From that point on, the clock has been handed down from eldest son to eldest son. Today, the still-intact, nearly two-hundred-year-old clock is owned by Gene Zachary, of Transylvania County. Wouldn't Colonel Zachary be pleased?

GENEVA'S EDEN

In 1954, the Cashiers Valley estate of T.R. Zachary was finally settled and his six children were each entitled to a portion of the old Zachary property. His granddaughters in Atlanta, Geneva Zachary Gibson and her sister Julia Luckie Zachary Bowers, were thrilled to divide the ten acres of Cashiers land originally intended for their deceased father, John A. Zachary. Their Aunt Bird Zachary Raines moved back to Cashiers after years in California to claim her portion of land, on which she immediately began building a home. This inspired Geneva to build herself a tiny unfinished cabin, using the same carpenters who were building Aunt Bird's home nearby. Geneva's little four-room cabin was dried in, the fireplace and chimney were completed, 110 volt electricity was hooked up, two sets of bunk beds were built in the bedroom and running water, ice cold, was piped in from the spring up the hill—gravity fed. There was no water heater, but a four-burner wood cookstove was put in with a large oven below and warming ovens above the burners. For fifty years, Geneva had been staying with kinfolk when she visited Cashiers and now, finally, she had her own place, humble as it was.

Furnishings were needed, so family members donated odds and ends of old pieces of mismatched furniture. There was a sofa that pulled out into a bed; an eclectic assortment of heavy pots and pans suitable for wood-stove cooking; Granny Viola's large kitchen cabinet that held what was left of a blue willow dish set; silverware in many patterns; a large grouping of "no-two-alike" glasses; and meal, flour, sugar, spices and canned goods. Uncle Grady's handmade wooden chest stood in the corner, filled with bed linens, including eleven family-made quilts and an old feather mattress.

Someone's much-used kitchen table surrounded by a number of interesting donated chairs completed the living/dining room, except for four Brumby rockers that were always taken outside into the front yard, along with their memories of having rocked several generations of children.

The small bathroom was plumbed with the usual fixtures one would expect to see, plus there were racks of towels of many sizes and colors, a few even embossed with the name of some unknown hotel. When you turned on the faucets, you got powerfully surging freezing water with sometimes a salamander popping out after his ride through the pipes all the way down from the spring. Unless you heated water on the wood stove and brought it in with you to the bathroom, you would shiver from the cold and vacate the bathroom quickly. In the tiny kitchen, there was not much more than a miniature kitchen sink and a galley-type refrigerator that would run on 110 volt electricity—no ice cubes.

"Geneva's Eden" cabin in Cashiers, built by Geneva Zachary Gibson in 1954–55. It burned to the ground in 1975. *Jane Gibson Nardy*.

Last on the list, Geneva decided, was a name for her cabin. She told her co-workers at Fort McPherson, her bridge club buddies and the members of her Sunday school class to submit a name for her mountain home, and whomever came up with the best name would win a vacation week there. These friends had been hearing weekly details of the progress of the construction, so they were very excited to be included in choosing a name for the cabin. Geneva actually already knew she wanted it named "Geneva's Eden," so she secretly told one friend to turn in that name. Entries for the contest came in and soon Geneva called the contestants together and announced the winner was "Geneva's Eden." Until now, only family members were aware that there was hanky-panky at the ballot box.

HISTORY OF THE
ZACHARY REUNION

A few Zachary cousins got together in the early 1900s to organize
a yearly Cashiers Zachary family reunion of the descendants of
Colonel John Alexander Zachary and his wife Sarah Roberts Zachary.
Prominent in this planning group were Tom Dillard and T.R. Zachary,
Cashiers residents and John R. Zachary of nearby South Carolina. One
of the earliest families to settle Cashiers Valley, the oldest members of the
first Zachary generation were fast dying out. By the time the first reunion
took place on August 28, 1909, at the Lower Zachary Cemetery in
Cashiers, only daughter Matilda Zachary Hinkle remained alive, having
outlived her thirteen brothers and sisters. Many of her siblings, including
Alfred Zachary, Thomas Jefferson Zachary, Ansylvania Zachary, Elizabeth
Zachary Allison and Susannah Zachary Norton, now rested nearby in the
cemetery. In attendance at the gathering, besides eighty-four-year-old
Matilda Hinkle, were sixteen grandchildren, thirty great-grandchildren
and twenty-eight great-great-grandchildren of the old pioneer couple.

On that first reunion day, Reverend W.T. Hawkins, known as "the
shepherd of the hills," led off the program with a prayer. While the children
played hide-and-seek in the nearby woods, and before the picnic baskets
were opened and the greatly anticipated contents set out upon the tables, a
lengthy speech was delivered by John R. Zachary Sr. of Seneca. He began
the Zachary saga in 1700, continued on with the arrival of Colonel John

and his children in the valley circa 1833 and then brought the story up to date, telling of the subsequent spread of the family from coast to coast. There was an unveiling of a monument to Colonel and Mrs. John Zachary that was placed over their graves. It was a lovely day spent at the cemetery, where old ties were renewed and a dinner on the grounds was shared.

A tradition had been born, and through the ensuing year, the family, their friends and neighbors continued to meet each August to honor the early Zacharys. In the year 1912, Robert Young Zachary of Baltimore, Maryland, a grandson of Colonel Zachary, gave an inspiring reunion speech that was reprinted in 1926 in the *Ruralite*. Since R.Y. Zachary had spent his childhood in the home of his Zachary grandparents, he had detailed stories of the twilight years of Colonel and Mrs. Zachary and offered firsthand insight into their personalities. At the age of seventy-five, with a steady hand on his old-fashioned steel and flint rifle, the colonel could shoot a squirrel's head off nine times out of ten. His wife had a keen appreciation of the ridiculous, and well into her old age she could be heard laughing with the hilarity of a schoolgirl. She kept "cheerfully busy with the flax wheel and distaff, the spinning wheel and hand loom."

Once again this year, on Sunday, August 24, 2008, the Zachary family will gather in Cashiers at high noon, under the picnic shed at the Lower Zachary Cemetery. This will be the hundredth Zachary Reunion. Just like the old days, everyone is invited to attend. All that is required is a food contribution for the picnic, a hearty appetite and a jolly disposition. Please join us.

Descendants of T.R. Zachary gathered at the Lower Zachary Cemetery at the 1977 Zachary family reunion. *Jane Gibson Nardy.*

BOUNTIFUL LIVING IN NORTON—1880 STYLE

D r. James Madison Zachary of Cashiers married pretty, young Alice Rodgers in 1877, and they initially set up housekeeping in a cabin near his relatives in Cashiers Valley. But with grander plans in mind, a large amount of land was soon purchased by the couple in the Norton area, and while Alice went about producing some little ones, husband Jim went about clearing land and building a fine house for the new family. His favorite brother, T.R. Zachary, was struggling to homestead out in Kansas, and Jim longed for his return. The following letter that Jim wrote on Christmas Day 1880 was obviously designed to lure his brother back to North Carolina and is filled with humorous descriptions of life on "easy street" in Jackson County.

> *To: Mr. T.R. Zachary, Olney, Kansas*
> *From: Cashiers Valley, N.C., Dec. 25 1880*
> *Dear Brother and Sister,*
>   *As the snow is about 12" deep and I can do nothing else I will try to write to you. I commenced about 3 months ago to write and to dreading it as I have almost entirely abandoned the idea of writing. I do not know why it is I cannot write. I have let all my Business go over the board that requires writing. I have been so busy since I came here that I have*

not had time to write to anybody as I have not wrote to C.C. [older brother, Christopher Columbus Zachary who was living in Kansas], *nor E.B.* [sister Eliza Belle Zachary who was living in Kansas], *Arlina* [sister Martha Arlena Zachary Courtney who was living in Kansas] *nor none of them yet.*

I came here 3 years ago to where Courtney [brother-in-law] *lived with the expectations of doing a big thing. So I have made a little start at raising children and some other stock. Well I will tell you how I commenced it. I just cleared and fenced 45 acres in the valley on the mountain between Father's and Bennet's. It is now sown in Timothy grass and chestnut trees. It joins fences with Father's and Bennet's and the Courtney place. 10 rails by with a locust stake in every corner. So then I concluded that it was too small a place for me.*

I then went to Hamburg [Township where Norton was located] *and bought 1,500 acres of land in one body around the Grassey Camp* [Norton] *and went to work on it. I first divided off 400 acres and have cleared and fenced 15 and it is now in grass and small grain. At the least there is 20 acres in wheat and rye plowed and sewn 10 inches deep, harrowed 2 times and brushed 2. Looks very pretty. Made 42 bushels of rye last year on 1 ½ bushels of seed on 3 acres, 40 bushels of wheat on 5 acres but sewn too thin. I only planted 1 acre in corn. It is in new ground and made 35 bushels and has 5 bushels yet. I have 25 hay stacks yet.*

I bought 1 hog from D. Norton. Now I have 35 head and have killed 10 heretofore which has made me about 1,200 lbs of pork and I have never fed them more than 1 bushel of corn nor nothing else. I have 10 head of cattle and have kept them on pasture winter and summer and haven't fed them yet until today and will have to feed them as long as this snow stays. There was no snow last winter nor winter before. I have 2 head of horses that I do not feed at all; only since the snow I gave them some hay.

I am in such good heart that I have set out 2,500 apple trees since I came here, of good fruit all…grafts, 1000 limber twigs. I have bought me a good new Champion mowing machine. Built 2 fish ponds. One covers 20 acres, the other 85 acres. I have also built me a splendid sawmill on Grassey Camp—cost $550—a good machine shop attached with turning lathe, circular saw, jig saw, shingle machine, planeing machine and grind stone all by the water. But I have not built yet tho I have my lumber all sawed and most of it to the place. I am building at the lower end of my new field, just south of where I now

The Norton, North Carolina house of Dr. James M. Zachary, which he described in his 1880 letter to T.R. Zachary. The house still stands in fine condition. *Jane Gibson Nardy.*

live about 400 yards and 400 yards above the ford of Grassey Camp. I am building 8 by 16 ft. rooms, 2 storys high, 3 chimneys, 6 fires and will commence in 3 weeks.

Yes, I have 3 dogs, 2 hounds and 1 young Tirk of the old plot stock right about 100 lbs., 8 grown cats, 7 pigeons and 2 girl babys. They are very fine baby girls. 1 is 2 years old and the other 10 months old. The oldest is named Elinora, the other Daisy Deen. There has been about 25 families moved in here since I have come, within 3 miles. You would not know the country hardly. I used to did not love farming but now I like it best of all. I am not doing much in the line of dentistry now as I think I can live on grass, fruit, fish and saw dust. I can catch 2 trout a minute from 6 to 16 inches long without a hook. You may talk of your new country and I have traveled over 9 states but I believe this to be the best lazy man's country in the world and it is fully as advantageous for an industrious man. It is true that we have but little money here. The reason is that we do not use it for currency and another thing is that we have no use for it as we have everything that we need.

I was very sorry that I could not send you the money you wanted me to last fall as I could not possibly get it. My taxes was about $85 and it was all I could do to get it up without leaving home and go off and work for it and that I had to do to pay my tax, but I hope the time will be soon when I will not have to leave at all. If I could sell off all my other lands which is about 2,300 acres then I would not have so much tax to pay and I now have a pretty good chance to do it.

Cole and Coffee and A.W. is doing merchant in Walhalla. Laura Hill and Charley has quit. Columbus Wilson and Thomas Wilson's girl married. Big Clum and James Hooper's girl married. Buris Norton and Lena Wilson married. Nany Allison did not wait to get married and neither did Julian Hedden. Nany Hill is married. July Bryson and Marion Wright is to marry today or tomorrow. Nobody died since you left but Uncle Elx Wilson.

All of our folks is well. We have not had a minutes' sickness in my family since I lived here. I hope these lines will find you both well. I would like to see you all so much.
Write soon, J.M. Zachary.

History Speeches

BURIED HISTORY AT THE
VILLAGE GREEN

How many of you folks here have ever accidentally dug up what could be called a buried treasure? Three years ago, at the Village Green at the Cashiers Crossroads, this is what actually happened to Marcia Moore and John McCarley. They were cleaning out trash from the marshy area near the wooden walkway that extends from the picnic pavilions over the marsh to the Cashiers Post Office. Lo and behold, under decades of leaves and mosses and lichens, they pulled up a metal chamber pot with a wire handle and a top. Surprised and curious, they pulled off the top, which was so rusted it disintegrated in their hands, and inside they found a bunch of old letters in remarkably good condition. Most of the letters were without their envelopes, but the few envelopes that were found were addressed to Mrs. D.C. Picklesimer at either Whiteside Cove or Grimshaws, North Carolina, and the earliest date was 1898.

Marcia and John scratched their heads for a while, wondering at the identity of the people who wrote and received these letters, and finally they contacted the Cashiers Historical Society. The pot and the letters ended up with me, and I was asked to find out who were the people in the letters and how in the world did the chamber pot get into the marsh.

I can tell you are wondering what qualified me to be trusted with this task. My formal training in tracing people both dead and alive came from studies in genealogy research—at universities, workshops, national conferences and finally formal testing to get my certification in that field. Prior to that, I had developed some rather unconventional skills that aided me later in life. First, in the 1960s, when I was in my twenties, I was hired as a skiptracer for the C&S National Bank's credit card department. My job was to telephone people who weren't making payments on their credit card bill. Some were just plain deadbeats, but many had real sad stories that would break your heart. I would take time to listen and was respectful and kind while asking for at least a token amount of money. There were no laws at that time to limit what a collector could do, so I would take accounts home with me at night and over the weekend and phone them at weird times. We had crisscross phone directories that enabled you to see the names and phone numbers of neighbors, so when someone didn't have a phone, or always avoided coming to the phone, I'd call a neighbor, tell them I owed the target person money and they would run next door and bring the person back to talk to me. I became the top collector in the department and no customer ever got mad, as I was so nice to them.

My other opportunity to trace people came via my dear late husband who had only one fault—he was a serial philanderer. He just couldn't help it. He could make up wonderful, creative explanations as to where he had been for days, but far on down the line I decided to check out some of his stories and, thanks to my skiptracing experience, he got busted. This was not a skill that I could put on a resume, but I sure learned a lot about being an amateur detective.

So here I was a few years ago with a chamber pot full of unsolved riddles. The first thing to do was open up the letters and place each page in protective plastic covers. Some of the letters consisted of just one page, while others had as many as eight pages. Next, I photocopied each page and then arranged the letters in chronological order. All but one of the letters was written from Sapphire, North Carolina, a place not to be confused with Sapphire Valley, which a hundred years ago had the name of Fairfield. The settlement of Sapphire was just over the Jackson County line in Transylvania County, and that area is located off of Highway 64, just behind the Sapphire Lakes development. The Sapphire Post Office was located across the road from today's Whisper Lake. There was one letter written from Douglas, Wyoming, but I'll discuss that letter last.

The recipient of the letters was Shellie Miller Picklesimer, who, with her husband "Dee" and several young children, lived in Whiteside Cove, close to Horse Cove. Shellie was the eldest of the three children of Alfred

The Miller home in old Sapphire, Transylvania County, North Carolina, where Shellie Miller Picklesimer was born and raised. *Jane Gibson Nardy*.

Henry Miller of Sapphire, and it was mainly her sister, Canty, and her brother, Napoleon, who were writing to her. The Sapphire area was knee deep in Millers, as Shellie's grandfather, Henry Woodfin Miller, had sired twenty-two children by two wives. There may have been even more children except that Henry died at the age of ninety-seven.

The surname of Picklesimer is undoubtedly known by all of you here. It was another early and prolific area family that is still populating Western North Carolina. Two of Shellie's daughters married brothers Ed and Fred Edwards of Highlands whose names are found in Ran Shaffner's *History of Highlands*.

What did Canty and Napoleon Miller write about to their sister Shellie? They were still teenagers in 1898 when the letters commenced, and they dearly missed their older sister who had married and left the nest. Each letter referred to how soon could they get together, either at Sapphire or Whiteside Cove. Canty wrote much longer letters than did Napoleon, and her spelling and grammar were superior. Their last dated letter (a few were undated) was in 1904, so we're looking at a short, six-year time span. During this period, Napoleon went away to school at Brevard Academy and his spelling and grammar noticeably improved.

As in letters throughout the ages, the state of everyone's health was discussed. They didn't have to worry about such things as AIDS or obesity, and vaccines and antibiotics were unknown to them. They dreaded outbreaks of typhoid, something awful called "the itch," smallpox, rabies, measles, whooping cough and mumps. Their teeth hurt and their boils were painful. They mentioned a preacher coming from Greenville to the mountains to hold revivals. While in Sapphire, he ate Sunday dinner with a family, and midway through the meal, he collapsed unconscious into his dinner plate. It was smallpox, and everyone who had shaken his hand at the meetings was in a state of panic. His fate was unknown, but Canty said if they could get their hands on him, they would kill him. Almost every letter spoke of the poor health of both Canty and her mother. They were weak, couldn't get out of bed and were too ill to make a visit or entertain company. Whatever Canty suffered from, it took away her life in 1903, when she was only twenty-two. Her mother lived to be eighty-six, and when she died in 1932, her obituary said she had been bedridden for thirty years. There weren't many doctors around. Canty wrote that a twelve-year-old boy near Toxaway got sick, but since it took the doctor so long to get there from Cashiers Valley, he died in just twenty-four hours.

Weather was not mentioned as much as I expected, but there were some weather details. Late one April, there came a severe cold snap accompanied by deep snow. They called it a "New Winter" and worried that some of their early plantings would be killed. The Millers evidently grew a variety of fruits such as apples, watermelons, grapes and peaches. Late one summer, Canty wrote that it was time to work on preserving the fruit for winter. They would dry some and can some and she dreaded it so much.

Canty was evidently a good seamstress and made clothes for Shellie and her children.

1899, Shellie, I have been doing some of your sewing today. I have it all finished but the bonnets. Are you going to put little Deroy in short dresses? Two of the dresses I have made look as if they were made for him.

In my home, when I was a child, there was a photograph of my father as a two-year-old standing barefoot in front of his Illinois farmhouse with his parents. He was wearing a short dress. He told us that when he was little, he was a girl, but he grew up to be a boy. It sounded logical to us. This was exactly the same time period that short dresses were being made for DeRoy Picklesimer.

Other kinds of sewing mentioned were quilt pieces for "memory quilts," knitting, spinning and weaving. Some of the other garments mentioned were corset covers, drawers with trimming, underskirts, waists (blouses), riding skirts, plain skirts and a type of scarf called "fascinators." (I found the meaning of that word in an old dictionary.)

Brother Napoleon played an April Fool's joke on the family, telling them that a couple in the neighborhood had run off across the state line and gotten married. The family fell for it and he let them discuss it for a whole day before he said, "April Fool." One spring day, just at dawn, a flock of wild ducks swooped down and landed on the Miller Pond and Napoleon shot six of them. Nothing else was mentioned about hunting. As for Napoleon's fate, he lived to be seventy-seven years old and died in Brevard, where he had served several terms as clerk of the Superior Court of Transylvania County. He fathered several children, one of whom was superintendent of Buncombe County Schools.

The Miller farm was alive with domesticated animals, and they were frequently mentioned, often by name. There was a horse named Toby. The blacksmith put on one of her shoes too tightly and made her temporarily lame. Papa's mare was attacked by bats and died. There were lots of chickens, and the family seemed to have a special fondness for guineas. Mother hogs had lots of piglets. The dog, Rover, bit Napoleon. Luck, the good cow, was sick for several weeks and then died from an unknown ailment. There were several cats, pet rabbits and squirrels and a calf that was bottle fed. Let's not forget the ducks and geese.

Frequently mentioned were Sunday school and church meetings and conferences, but there's no mention of God or morality. In fact, in one letter, Canty was telling Shellie who was dating whom or who had recently married, and she quite casually wrote, "I guess you know Sus Siler. She is married now. She married Dan Walker. She had four children before she was married."

I would like to offer you my theory on how the chamber pot full of letters got buried at the Village Green. Where it was found was way out behind the home of Edith Picklesimer Passmore, one of the daughters of Shellie Miller Picklesimer. The letters were surely special to Shellie because they were about all she had to remind her of her little sister, Canty, who died so young. Next, the letters came into possession of Edith Passmore sometime after the death of her mother, Shellie, in 1950, and perhaps they were stored in the back of the Passmore's garage, which sat very close to today's Village Green. Then someone at sometime decided to clean out the garage and *wham*, out went the chamber pot—thrown in back, behind the garage, where it remained for years, gradually sinking down and getting covered each year by more and more leaves.

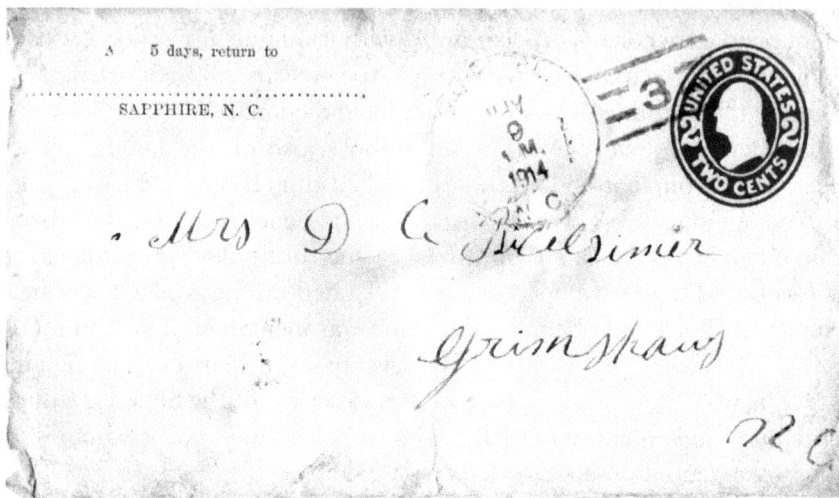

An envelope with the stamped date of 1914, addressed to Mrs. D.C. (Shellie) Picklesimer, Grimshaws, North Carolina. She was the postmaster. *Margaret Passmore Glance.*

Now, let me tell you about the letter written to Shellie from Douglas, Wyoming. It was dated July 1908, and was written by Sallie Bryan Edwards, wife of Willie Edwards. They had gone from this area to homestead in Wyoming along with many of their neighbors. Frances Lombard's book, *From the Hills of Home in Western North Carolina,* devotes five chapters to that move west and Tom Picklesimer discusses it at length in his book *My Life and Times.* As a young man he was part of that migration.

That day in July, Sallie Edwards indicated a longing to return to the North Carolina mountains. She mentioned many living near her in Wyoming who were also from the Cashiers/Highlands area, familiar surnames such as Lombard, Franks and Alexander. She wrote about her activities—canning beans, beets and rhubarb—and how her potatoes weren't doing so well, and in town, potatoes were selling at seven cents a pound. She had a nice lot of little chickens—about a hundred and growing so nicely. She had not been to town for months, and she said her husband Willie was away up on the high plains with the sheep. She closed the letter saying it was time for her to milk the cows.

Willie Edwards remained in Douglas, Wyoming, until at least 1930, as he was listed on the 1930 Wyoming census with his wife Sallie and six children. But by 1940, he was living in Highlands, married to Minnie Zoellner. He had deserted Sallie and the six children. He owned the Old

Edwards Inn, became mayor of Highlands and was featured in "A Walk in the Park" a few years ago, but no mention was made of his former life in Wyoming. His first wife, Sallie, remained in Douglas and is buried in the town cemetery, as are many others originally from these parts. One of Willie's descendants, with whom I have corresponded, is presently serving as a Wyoming state senator.

Last month I led a tour for the Cashiers Historical Society based on the major families found in the letters. The next week, there was an article about the tour in the *Crossroad's Chronicle*. I got a phone call late that night from a man who used to live in Cashiers but is now living in Charlotte. He said a friend had called him and told him about the newspaper article and about the old letters found buried at the Village Green. He asked me, "What was the date on those letters?" When I told him they ran from 1898 to around 1908 he said, "Whew, I was scared they were some hot love letters I wrote in the 1950s to a girl who lived near the Village Green, and if my wife found out about that, she'd kill me."

The old lover's name shall remain anonymous.

LIFE IN NINETEENTH-CENTURY WESTERN NORTH CAROLINA

My assignment tonight is to discuss what life was like in the Western North Carolina mountains in the 1800s. This is to prepare you for the William Holland Thomas Symposium offered by the Cashiers Historical Society on May 5, 6 and 7, 2005. Colonel Thomas's life span was 1805 to 1893. His life was shaped by the place and time of his birth, and then he personally played a big part in shaping early mountain life.

Is anyone here from the newspaper? I have become wary of being quoted. I recently spoke to the Highlands Rotary about the symposium and told them some of my favorite things about William Holland Thomas. Speaking about his mental struggles near the end of his life, I told of his being confined to an asylum for a year before being returned home. I said he was lucid most of the time but sometimes had outbursts of violence aimed at his wife so that she had to build a rock room to house him on those dark days. A few sentences later, I mentioned his wife's death at age forty-five and that when she died, her brothers immediately sent Thomas back to the asylum for good.

Here is what was written in the newspaper, "He returned home from the asylum and abused his wife until she died in 1877 at the age of 45." That is not what I said. Now I can sympathize with politicians who always complain about being quoted "out of context."

Here, today, I'll touch on a few subjects about life in the 1800s, such as: Who lived here? How did they get from one place to another? What were the schools like? How did folks make a living? What were the political issues? Where did families go to shop? And, what was it like to live without electricity? I'm going to fudge a bit and concentrate on life in Cashiers Valley.

Our area was not always considered prime land. It loomed as a harsh, inaccessible place, and on maps it appeared to be too steep to farm. White settlers first chose to homestead in wide, flat valleys dissected by strong running streams and containing plenty of fertile soil.

After the land was opened for settlement, following the 1819 treaty with the Cherokee, a survey was made by Colonel Robert Love in 1820 where lots were laid out, usually in 640-acre parcels. It was not until the mid-1820s that the Barak Norton family made its way from nearby South Carolina into Whiteside Cove. All their belongings were loaded onto pack horses that made their way up what was described as a "wilderness trail."

Less than ten years after the Nortons came, the Zachary family moved from Surry County, North Carolina, into what was to become Cashiers Valley. Both the Nortons and the Zacharys applied for and received many land grants from the State of North Carolina. The Zacharys' trip from Surry County, which bordered the state of Virginia, is an often-told tale, as remembered by Elizabeth Zachary Allison after she became an adult. At the first Zachary reunion in 1909, she spoke of the early 1830s trip:

> At that time there were no roads through this valley—nothing but Indian trails from the foot of the mountains on the South Carolina side to the Tuckaseegee. Think of us winding our way up the Chattooga, cutting our way into this valley, surrounded on every side by the wild beasts of the forest.

Humankind used the ancient animal trails to first navigate the mountain terrain. Those paths were well worn by elk, bears, panthers, deer and even herds of buffalo. Many sites, rivers and passes were named for the presence of the buffalo and those names remain today.

In George Ellison's column, "Back Then," in the November 17–23, 2004 issue of the *Smoky Mountain News*, he described the death, in 1799, of the last buffalo in Western North Carolina. It took place at Bull Creek, located along today's Blue Ridge Parkway, north of Asheville. A hunter shot the old bull buffalo with a muzzleloading rifle. So, when the white settlers first came into the Cashiers area, they only missed the buffalo by about thirty years.

In 1848, William Holland Thomas, who was this area's representative at the North Carolina legislature in Raleigh, introduced a petition to construct the Tuckaseigee–Keowee Turnpike. It would run from the

Cherokee area, through Cashiers Valley and on into South Carolina to the Keowee River. Well-known citizens who lived along the route signed the petition, including Alexander Zachary of Cashiers. The original petition can be found in the William Holland Thomas papers in the Museum of the Cherokee. The professor, who recently transcribed these papers and journals, will be one of the speakers at the symposium.

In 1864, a union soldier named W.H. Shelton, with a few of his army friends, made a stealthy journey from Walhalla, South Carolina, up into the valley, roughly following the Turnpike Road. You see, they had escaped a Confederate prison and were aiming for the Union lines in East Tennessee. Long after the war was over, Shelton's story, "A Hard Road Out of Dixie," appeared in the book *Famous Adventures and Prison Escapes of the Civil War*. In the middle of December, it took Shelton and his men two days to reach Cashiers.

> *We struggled up the foot-hills and outlying spurs of the mountain, through an uninhabited waste of rolling barrens, along an old stage road, seemingly long deserted, and in places impassable to a saddle-mule. We followed this stage road through the scattering settlement of Cashier's Valley in Jackson County, North Carolina.*

This group was headed to a house in Norton, where they expected to get help, but they were captured before they reached their goal.

A firsthand account of how transportation had progressed by 1877 can be found in a letter from Alexander Zachary to his son, T.R. Zachary, written from Cashiers Valley to Rush County, Kansas, where T.R. was attempting to homestead in a Soddy house. The letter described a week-long adventure by wagon through deep snows and slippery ice from Walhalla, South Carolina, to Cashiers Valley. It is hard for any of us to imagine it taking a week to go from Walhalla to Cashiers.

About ten years after Alexander's icy trip from Walhalla, an ornithologist at Harvard named William Brewster traveled through parts of Western North Carolina. George Ellison's *Smoky Mountain News* article of just a few weeks ago told of the journal Brewster kept on his mid-1880s journey, which included an interesting passage pertaining to the road from Highlands, through Cashiers Valley, to East LaPorte. The party left Highlands at 9:00 a.m. and didn't reach East LaPorte, which is located on Highway 107 just a few miles this side of Western Carolina University, until sunset. This was a trip of eight or nine hours, one that today takes forty-five minutes tops. Brewster said:

The road was an almost continual descent and for about six miles below Hamburg [today's Glenville] *it was steep, rocky and dangerous, barely six inches from the brink of a precipice with the Tuckaseigee River roaring and rushing in white foam over the rapids, hundreds of feet below. The scenery was superb with the picturesque river, the vertical walls of the canyon and innumerable falls; Rhododendron-clad banks and grand old woods multiplying the attractions and giving a never ending variety to the landscape. The forests were the finest we have thus far seen with many of the oaks and tulip trees exceeding five feet in diameter with straight column-like trunks.*

The terrible condition of the roads was a common theme of complaints. There was just so much a crew of conscripted workers could do with a couple of mules, a slip pan and shovels. During the winter and early spring, freezes, thaws, snow and rain turned roads into hazardous mud pits. A few months later, with dry weather, dust became the enemy.

Now, let's move on to the very end of the 1800s, when the first hotel in the Cashiers area, the Fairfield Inn, was completed in Fairfield, now called Sapphire Valley. In one of John Parris's columns in the *Asheville Citizen Times,* he quoted Cashiers resident Walter Fugate:

Folks would come by train to Toxaway, which was about 12 miles or so from Fairfield and I'd haul 'em the rest of the way. Hauled 'em in those old time surreys. I'd make a trip to Toxaway once a day. The train came in about 11 a.m. and I'd get back to the hotel about 2:30 or 3:00 in the afternoon. Folks that had to catch the train had to get up mighty early. It left out of Toxaway at 7 a.m. and we'd leave the inn here about 4:00 a.m. in the morning.

Mountain schooling was very much a hit and miss proposition in the 1800s, partly due to the relatively small population. *The History of Jackson County*, published by the Jackson County Historical Association, says that in 1851, when Jackson County was formed from Macon County, free textbooks and college educated teachers were unheard of. To the majority of people in Western North Carolina, school meant little more than learning enough to read the Bible and "go through" the blue-back speller. School terms were short—only one to four months—buildings borrowed (only one room was needed) and textbooks were often limited to one or two books for the entire school.

Here in Cashiers Valley, the earliest school talked about was the one established by the Hampton sisters, located across from the Hampton estate. There doesn't seem to be a firm date for the beginnings of that school, but since the Hampton's first purchase of Cashiers land was in 1855, it was certainly after the mid-1800s. There were a few primary sources available about the early school experiences of children in Western North Carolina. Will Thomas, who was born in 1805 in the general area of Waynesville, was purported to be educated entirely by his mother. He certainly learned enough to be able to read a whole set of law books by his early teens.

Flora Zachary, who was born in 1856 at today's Zachary-Tolbert House, was the daughter of Mordecai Zachary and Elvira Keener Zachary. Many years later, after Flora's husband had died, she wrote what she called her "autobiography" and told a little about attending school in Cashiers.

> *I went to school in Cashiers Valley—to the fall school—which held for a term of four months each year. The teacher boarded at Uncle Bill Norton's.*

I figure she would have started school in about 1862. Flora must have received a firm educational foundation as she later graduated from college and taught school herself.

We'll go back to Kansas now, to the approximate year of 1878, where T.R. Zachary, age twenty-eight, wrote a letter to his fiancé in Georgia.

> *I have seven sisters, all married but one; there are four brothers and I am the only single one of the boys. My father is living and is now about 74 years old and it has only been three years since he married the second time.*
>
> *You must look over this, my awkwardness in writing, tis so seldom that I write. I am almost out of practice—don't know whether you can read this or not. No doubt you have found that I was not competent of writing and composing in good English. Well, there are two causes. One is because I am careless and another is a lack of an education. Still, the latter was not my fault. I was unfortunate to be about 10 years old when the war broke out [Civil War] and I was the only boy left to take care of my afflicted parents and 3 or 4 sisters, so you can readily see that during the years of war, all possibilities for schooling were done away with and I was the only help my father had for three years after the war or until he was able to see to the farm himself. Thus you can see that I was out of school for about seven years during my best school days. Still, I have learned enough by observation to take the place of considerable book learning.*

Judging from Flora and T.R's writings, there was a school in Cashiers Valley in the 1860s with a boarding teacher, although the school was only in session about four months a year.

Jumping ahead to the end of the 1800s, my grandfather, John A. Zachary, attended grammar school in Cashiers and then went to Cullowhee High School, also called Cullowhee Academy. When he graduated from the Teacher's Normal Division of the school in 1898, he was already occasionally teaching the lower grades in the Cashiers school. One of his teachers was Professor Robert L. Madison, who was instrumental in turning the school at Cullowhee into Western Carolina University. It does seem that it was possible to receive a fine education in these mountains in the nineteenth century.

The next topic will cover the question: Where did the folks in the 1800s go shopping for the things they could not produce themselves? In the earliest times, there were trading posts, and Will Thomas owned a whole string of them through the mountains. At the upcoming symposium, George Frizzell, head of special collections at the Hunter Library at Western Carolina University, will enlighten us with a discussion of "Store Ledgers in Western North Carolina—Thomas and Businesses in the 19th Century." George is a native of Jackson County, descended from an old founding family, and he has at his fingertips in the library a huge collection of records that relate to the area's early settlement. He puts together a great speech, and you won't want to miss his presentation.

When the Nortons and Zacharys first moved into Whiteside Cove and Cashiers Valley, there was no post office, and their mail came to Pickens Courthouse, South Carolina. It then got up the mountains the best way it could, usually in the care of a resident who had gone to do some shopping in Pickens. I have an envelope that is dated 1836, addressed to "Col. John A. Zachary, Pickens Courthouse, South Carolina," and in the bottom left-hand corner is written, "Please deliver to Cashier's Valley." It would be 1839 before the U.S. Postal Service officially established the post office of Cashiers Valley.

Throughout the 1800s, the habit of local residents making the trip to South Carolina to shop continued. Surviving from 1840 is a receipt from the E.E. Alexander Store, Pickens Courthouse, South Carolina, made out to the Misses Zachary. They had purchased, "Muslin, Calico, Bonnetts and Draping, Shirting, Edging, Cups, Handkerchiefs and Shoes." And remember that icy trip that Alexander Zachary and his wife made from Walhalla to Cashiers in 1877? They had been shopping. In that same 1877 letter to his son, while telling him what was happening around town,

Alexander mentioned, "We have two stores in the Valley. Your Uncle Jonathan and a man by the name of Cline has them."

Some families, in the fall, would take a wagon full of their farm products, such as apples, cabbages, potatoes and chestnuts, to the market in South Carolina, and while there, they would stock up on the store-bought items they would need during the winter. After a day or so, they would come back up the mountain with a hundred pounds of flour, a hundred pounds of sugar and big tubs of shortening, and maybe some store-bought shoes for the children. Let me put a word in here about chestnuts. In the nineteenth century, the forests in Western North Carolina were completely dominated by the American chestnut tree. These huge trees furnished food for man and beast and were a resource for building houses. A time traveler from that era would not recognize today's forest landscape.

It seemed that every little town and settlement had at least one store, and it was common for the post office to be located in a store. People would come in to get their mail, buy a needed item or two and visit with the other folks coming in and out of the store. A general store made a good meeting place for the townsfolk.

We are fortunate here in Cashiers to have a rare store account ledger from the 1840s that has survived in fine condition. It is from the general store of Alexander Zachary and it gives us a marvelous picture of what kind of transactions went on in a typical small-town Western North Carolina store. There is a loose alpha-index in the front of the ledger to all the names of the individuals who traded at the store, most of whom had charge accounts. There is a date and description of the items purchased and a date and method

The home of William Norton and Suzannah Zachary Norton where drovers would stop for the night. The house still stands in Cashiers. *Jane Gibson Nardy.*

of payment. Some customers paid at the time of purchase, with cash, but more often, the purchases were paid by barter on the spot or at a later date.

Take into consideration how small the population of Cashiers Valley was in the 1840s. Counting the surrounding areas of Fairfield, which today is called Sapphire Valley, Toxaway and Hamburg, known today as Glenville, you were looking at a total population of three hundred, tops.

So, as Lorie Holter wrote in her introduction to *Alexander Zachary's Store Account Book* (unpublished), into Zachary's store on a typical day came the farmers from the scattered farms who, although self-sufficient, had little cash. They came to exchange news, collect personal debts and exchange their items at the store. They bought such things as salt, rum, shoe leathers, tobacco, coffee, cow bells, thread, sets of knives and forks, glass window panes, whiskey, smoothing irons, horseshoes, nails, sugar, skillets, picks and shovels. Many of the goods had been bought in South Carolina by Zachary and brought by wagon to Cashiers Valley to be sold in his store.

Other items were more likely to have been taken in by trade—ground meal, apples, bacon, butter, livestock, pigs, horses, cattle, turkeys, hams, beef, deer and bearskins, brooms, potatoes and venison. The bartering system really shows up strong when reading how customers repaid their debts to Zachary's store. In 1847, John Shattien settled his account of $2.62 with a bear hide. Thomas Woods paid his bill with 7½ deer skins.

Testimony to the usual deplorable condition of the roads can be seen where a man pays his bill with a few days' work on the road. E.L. Allison, who was Alexander Zachary's brother-in-law, shoed horses and worked on tools, like a mattock and plows, and Allison lent his wagon and horses for one day. John Fisher brought in venison hams and worked for Zachary six days. Items that the women had produced, like woven cloth and churned butter and cheese, were bartered.

Will Thomas, in one of his journals, said that on July 22, 1853, he "hired a young man to take me to Cashiers Valley." Three days later, still in Cashiers Valley, he mentioned a transaction he made with Alexander Zachary. He wrote:

> Got a horse of Alexander Zachary…went as far as Mr. Wilson on Cullowhee. Next day went on to John Messers. Sent horse back to Zacharys…Borrowed Messers and reach home in the night.

Lorie Holter, a graduate student from Western Carolina University, wrote a forty-page introduction to her transcription of the Cashiers store account book. Near the end of the introduction, she mused:

On any given day in the 1840s or 1850s, when Zachary was keeping his store ledger, a farmer could be seen walking along the dusty, rut laden main road, through Cashiers Valley. His oxen pulled a creaking load of cabbages, bacon, and butter that had been tended, cured, and churned by the members of his family.

As he neared the Zachary store his ears caught the sounds of commerce and community—the chortling mix of talk and loud laughter, the jingling of coinage changing hands and the squeal of multiple hogs confined in a pen awaiting their walk to the markets of South Carolina. The dewy air of the morning held the aroma of smoke tobacco, which filtered down the path to meet the farmer as he entered into the clamor of activity.

At the end of the century, in 1892, Evan Pell built himself a fine building, using American chestnut and English poplar for the siding. He opened a general store. You know the place today as the Cornucopia Restaurant. There are several structures around town that once housed a store, including the Hanks House, the Wormy Chestnut, the BP Service Station and the building where Lynn Holloway's Antique Shop used to be.

The earliest record of politics in Cashiers Valley can be found in the book *1835 Poll Books of North Carolina.* In that year's election, our area was in the Fairfield Precinct of Macon County. (Remember that we were part of Macon County until 1851.) Subtitled, "Election at Franklin for Congress," the name of Cashiers Valley is not shown at all, but under "Votes Given at Fairfield Precinct" are listed the names of the voters we know lived here. There were twenty-nine voters from Fairfield, including Barak and Elias Norton, who lived in Whiteside Cove; Alexander Wilson, who lived in Hamburg/ Glenville; John Stuart of Yellow Mountain; John and Alexander Zachary of Cashiers; as well as Moses Butler and members of the Reed, Lowe, Burrell and Dodgin families. We don't know how they voted or even who was on the ballot, but we do know these men took the time to exercise their right to vote.

Jackson County was formed in 1851 with the new town of Webster as the county seat. Daniel Webster had just died, and the naming of this town for him was a graceful concession to the Whig element of the county. Honoring "Old Hickory," Andrew Jackson, by naming the county for him, pleased the Democrats. The first senator from Jackson County was none other than William Holland Thomas.

During the Civil War, there was a great division in Western North Carolina between those for the Union and those for the Confederacy. Nowhere was the division more obvious than in the highest mountain areas like Cashiers Valley. It was the last part of the war when conditions were so desperate in the valley, with escaped Union soldiers appearing unexpectedly looking for help and with Union Colonel George Washington Kirk, from East Tennessee, swooping down on the mountain people in his infamous looting raids. Added to that mixture were the ever-increasing numbers of deserters from the Confederacy, hiding out in caves during daylight hours and slipping down the mountains to tend their crops at night.

T.R. Zachary, at age fourteen, helped lead Union soldiers who had escaped from South Carolina Confederate prisons to safety in Knoxville, Tennessee. Later in the century, he exchanged letters with one of those soldiers who had become an Illinois state senator. T.R. was known as the "Boy Guide." In a letter dated 1890, Senator Bassett of Peoria, Illinois, wrote to T.R., who had left his homesteading attempt in Kansas and was back home in Cashiers Valley.

> *Mr. Zachary, I was a Democrat too, before the war, but that war shot all the democracy out of me and now I am a strong Republican, so guess you and I better not talk politics.*

Hardly anyone had just one occupation in the mountains in the 1800s, although most recorded simply "farmer" when the census taker came around. The rest of the South was based on an economy that was derived from a single cash crop, while the mountain people's economy derived from a diversified agricultural base. Barbara Dooley, who published a transcription of the first Jackson County census, which was for the year 1860, gave this rundown on occupations. Among the white population, there were 917 farmers, 3 merchants, 6 carpenters, 2 saddlers, 4 doctors, 2 lawyers, 3 clerks, 1 surveyor, 4 millers, 1 blacksmith, 2 shoemakers, 5 mechanics, 2 Baptist ministers, 1 miner, 17 farm laborers, 1 tanner, 9 teachers, 2 Methodist ministers, 1 tailor, 1 sheriff and 8 households headed by women. The ministers very likely also farmed, and the farmers did a little blacksmithing and were handy as carpenters. The total white population was counted at 5,155, and there were 1,063 Native Americans.

No dentists were mentioned, but shortly after the end of the Civil War, James Madison Zachary, one of the sons of Alexander, studied to be a dentist in South Carolina and practiced that trade in Norton for the rest of his life. But that was not all he did, and we have evidence of that in a very enthusiastic and humorous letter he wrote in 1880 to his brother, T.R., who had by that time married his Georgia sweetheart and brought her to his little

Soddy house on the plains of Kansas. It would be impossible to describe Dr. James M. Zachary's occupation in a single word. He officially could have been listed as a dentist, but then he was also a farmer with multiple crops, a sawmill owner and a finished carpenter. Not to mention the crop of girls he eventually raised—eight in all of whom two became dentists.

The last subject today will be exploring mountain life prior to electricity. I first put together a speech on this topic last September for the members of the Cedar Creek Racquet Club. It was an after-lunch talk, so I was treated to a good meal. I clearly remember the date because it was my birthday, September 16, and outside the Racquet Club dining room window the wind was howling and sheets of rain were blowing sideways. It was the beginning of Hurricane Ivan's visit to the mountains, and when I finished talking about living without the luxury of electric lights, refrigeration and flushing toilets, the audience scurried home, and within six hours, the power was off and they were living a pioneer life without the skills of a pioneer.

Planning ahead was the cornerstone of nineteenth-century life. Most everything had to be done between sunrise and sunset, which made for short winter days and long summer days. Growing crops and then preserving some of the harvest for winter use was necessary. The places

T.R. Zachary's house, which was built in the early 1880s and was not wired for electric power until after World War II. *Jane Gibson Nardy.*

for food storage were usually in a basement or in a detached root cellar, sometimes called a bank house. Since it has now been around seventy-five years since the need for a root cellar vanished, they are seldom seen anymore, although on old farm grounds, you can sometimes still see one.

In closing, I'd like to tell you something about William H. Thomas that you'll probably not hear at the symposium. He was a real ladies' man, and although he was over age fifty before he settled down with a wife with whom he fathered three children, he had many earlier dangerous liaisons with both married and single women. He produced countless offspring this way, and those "Wood's Colts," as they are referred to in the mountains, were often named William or Thomas. In gathering records for my symposium talk on his connections with Cashiers Valley, Charlie and Jan Wyatt read some of Will Thomas's detailed diaries and gave me a list of dates he had visited the valley, noting with whom he had stayed. Scanning the list, I realized that Will Thomas in 1849 was possibly several times a visitor in the happy household of my great-great-grandparents, Alexander and Isabella Zachary. In 1850, my great-grandfather, T.R. Zachary was born, and guess what the "T" stood for? You got it—"Thomas." Now, I'm wondering if I should get a DNA test.

WILL THOMAS
SLEPT HERE

Not long after the land that encompasses today's Cashiers was made available for settlement, Will Thomas was exploring the area. *The History of Jackson County*, in its section on "The Pioneer Experience," states:

> *In the 1830s a group of businessmen, including Senator John C. Calhoun and William Sloan from South Carolina, promoted a scheme for a Cincinnati to Charleston Railroad across the Blue Ridge. They surveyed from the ridge dividing the Keowee and Little Rivers, across the Chattoga Ridge into Cashiers Valley where they ceased their efforts— realizing that the elevation was too great for the railroad.*

Since Will Thomas had met Senator John C. Calhoun in Washington, D.C., in 1831, and since both of these men were keen on building railroads, Thomas was surely involved in this venture and likely on the scene physically.

It was 1820 before our land here was opened for settlement, and when the Norton family, the earliest pioneer family, arrived in Whiteside Cove in the mid-1820s, this area was still Haywood County. In 1828, we became part of the new Macon County, which was carved out of Haywood County, and when Calhoun and Sloan and Thomas were surveying through this valley in the 1830s, it remained in Macon County. It wasn't until the end of 1851 that we became part of the new Jackson County.

CASHIERS HISTORICAL SOCIETY

presents a

Symposium

The Life and Times of

William Holland Thomas

May 5, 6, & 7, 2005

High Hampton Inn & Country Club
Cashiers, NC

portrait attributed to Jesse Atwood ca. 1850
Courtsey of the Museum of the Cherokee Indian

The front cover of the brochure for the Cashiers Historical Society's first symposium, 2005, entitled "The Life and Times of William Holland Thomas." *Cashiers Historical Society.*

One of the first houses in which Will Thomas slept in Cashiers Valley may have been McKinney's Boardinghouse. Thomas mentions the family and the house several times in his journals. The South Carolina McKinney family arrived in the 1830s, a little before or a little after the Zachary family, according to which story you believe. David U. Sloan published, in 1891, a book entitled *The Fogy Days and Now*, which included some of his childhood memories of visiting Cashiers Valley. He offers us a charming description of the McKinneys and their Cashiers boardinghouse.

> *The visitor, in ascending this mountain region, notices the wonderful change in the atmosphere, its bracing effect on the system, the feeling of freshness and delight experienced in this altitude. The effect on the appetite is remarkable; first keen and then ravenous.*
>
> *We can never forget our first visit to Cashiers Valley, our relish for old Aunt Sally McKinney's "yaller-legged" chickens, fried so brown, and floating in the golden melted butter, snow-white smothered cabbage, mealy Irish potatoes, cracking wide open as they were lifted from the kettle, buckwheat cakes and mountain honey, nor shall we try to erase from our memory old Mr. Mac's mountain dew that sat out on the water-shelf before and after and between meals.*

(I suspect High Hampton is still using Mrs. McKinney's recipe for fried chicken.)

The old McKinney house was torn down just a few decades ago. Anyone interested in seeing what the two-story, wooden structure looked like, can see a picture of it in the book *The Cashiers Area—Yesterday, Today, and Forever*, where it is called the Chris Rogers house. Also, the McKinney spring, where the mountain dew was kept, is still very much in evidence, just across the street from today's McKee Properties.

Moving on into the 1840s time frame, we learn from Thomas's journals that on June 4, 1842, while he was en route to Pendleton, South Carolina, for a meeting, he stopped at Colonel Zachary's. He was speaking of Colonel John Alexander Zachary, the Cashiers Zachary patriarch and the father of Mordecai Zachary, one of the colonel's fourteen children. The year 1842 was also the year that the descendants of Mordecai claim he started building his house, so it is quite possible that Thomas caught a glimpse of the twenty-year-old Mordecai felling a large tree or setting up his sawmill on the river.

Eight days after staying at the colonel's home, Thomas wrote that on June 12, 1842, during his return trip from Pendleton, he went to see

White Water Falls with Jesse McKinney, but the trail was lost, adding seven extra miles in the saddle. He probably spent the night once again in the valley, which, as you're beginning to see, was the logical place to stop on any journey from the Waynesville area to South Carolina. In South Carolina, there were the upstate markets, as well as the trains that could transport the mountain products to even more distant markets all over the South and the East Coast.

All the mountain farmers, and do remember that Will Thomas *was* a farmer, raised livestock for their own use and would often send a few head to the market for cash. There was an autumn market in South Carolina for the sale of livestock, and professional drovers from Haywood and even Buncombe Counties would buy the extra hogs, cattle and even turkeys from the farmers and drive them straight through Cashiers Valley into South Carolina.

The drovers needed a place to rest while their stock was fed and watered, and many homes in Cashiers were opened to accommodate this need. One of those places was the home of William Norton—a house that is standing today. The large Norton spring where the livestock drank is still visible just across Highway 107 South from the Norton house. It must have been quite a sight to have seen one of the livestock drives through the valley. I've seen a sketch of a drover, driving a herd of hogs along a winding, roller-coaster, dusty mountain dirt road. The hogs, fattened on a never-ending supply of rich chestnuts, looked like they were flowing over each hill, and you could imagine that their squealing could be heard from a distance. The name of the sketch was *This little piggy went to market*.

Getting land grants from the State of North Carolina was an important and often recurring event for mountain men in the 1840s, and it was a lengthy, detailed process. It is laid out for us in Leary and Stirwalt's book, *North Carolina Research*. First, there was the "Land Entry," in which a person made application to the land office for a chosen piece of vacant land that had not been previously granted.

Second, after the entry had been made, a warrant was issued by the secretary of state. In reality, this was an order to the county surveyor to survey and further describe the requested land. The third step was the "Plat of Survey," which was produced by the county surveyor and which required him to physically go out, personally survey the land and draw a small map or plat of the survey. This plat included the names of any owners of adjoining land and the names of the chain carriers. Often, the chain carriers were either relatives or neighbors of the person requesting the land. The last step was the "Patent," which was actually the official grant. A grant did not mean the land was free for the taking. Oh, no—the going rate in the 1840s was about five dollars for a hundred acres.

The time it took to get from step one to step four and official ownership of the land could take as long as three or four years. As soon as William Holland Thomas began his fourteen-year career as a member of the North Carolina state legislature, he was of help to his voters in speeding up the land grant process. In one of his journals, there was a section entitled, "Journal from General Assembly 1848." A subtitle read, "Grants obtained for constituents, 1848–49" Among the names listed were several members of the Cashiers Valley Zachary family. The first name was Alexander Zachary—who was getting Grant #797, consisting of a hundred acres for the price of $5.95. Then, five other Zachary names were listed, each receiving a hundred acres and each paying $5.95 for their land.

Another section of that journal was headed, "Indian Matters— Washington, DC." Thomas made a notation dated 1849 that read, "Hired Mr. Burt to help with Catawba Indian relations, South Carolina. He had been employed by Col. William Sloan before I came on."

We can speculate that the "Mr. Burt" might have been Armistead Burt, the second owner of the Zachary-Tolbert House, and Colonel William Sloan's name I've already mentioned as being a member of that 1830s surveying group looking for a railroad route through these mountains.

Sloan was also related to the David Sloan who wrote the book *The Fogy Days and Now*. The same names keep popping up, year after year, and Thomas knew them all.

As far as the future of Cashiers Valley was concerned, perhaps the most important document found in the papers of Will Thomas was the 1848 petition he presented to the North Carolina legislature for the building of a toll road through the valley. A few years ago, my late cousin, Jimmy Myers, a descendant of both the Norton and Zachary families, was helping with the newly acquired Thomas papers at the Museum of the Cherokee Indian. He would excitedly phone me after a day's work, with little tidbits he had learned about Thomas's activities—especially those that might pertain to our area. He made a point of making me a copy of a petition for the Tuckaseigee– Keowee Turnpike, knowing that it was the precursor of Highway 107, and seeing that it bore the signature of my ancestor, Alexander Zachary, as well as that of one of his ancestors. The turnpike was approved by the early part of the 1850s and individuals could buy shares in the company. The road started at "Fisher's Store," located in the northern part of Jackson County, and went "through Cashiers Valley to the South Carolina line." From there, it continued on to the Keowee River, with that section maintained by folks in South Carolina. An entry in Thomas's diary in October 1855 said, "Laying of the road," referring to the Tuckaseige–Keowee Turnpike. At last, the existing road through Cashiers was widened, improved and, although it needed constant repairs and was a daily subject to complaints, the dirt/gravel turnpike championed by Will Thomas remained much the same until it was straightened out and paved in the 1930s.

In the 1850s, there are many references in Thomas's diaries about Cashiers Valley. On July 21, 1850, he traveled to Cashiers Valley, where he stayed the night at William Barnes's home and had dinner with the McKinneys. We can make a good educated guess of what he ate there. The following day, on July 22, he said he "Spoke at Cashiers Valley, and stayed with Thompson Wilson." I've wondered about what the subject of that speech might have been and I'll bet it involved politics.

There's a brief mention of Thomas staying at a Zachary house in 1852, and that was the same year that Mordecai Zachary and his wife, Elvira Keener, married and moved into their house. The newlyweds took in boarders, but the only names documented as staying in the Zachary-Tolbert House were folks from South Carolina. However, I feel certain that Thomas did occasionally sleep in that house.

In July 1853, Thomas traveled to Charleston to attend a meeting about the Blue Ridge Railroad. On his return trip from Charleston to North Carolina, around the July 22, he wrote that he "hired a young man to take me to Cashiers Valley" and that he "reached Jonathan Zachary's about sundown." He had come by rail from Charleston to the South Carolina upstate, and from there he had hitched a ride up into the valley. The next day, on July 24, he simply wrote, "Remained with Zachary," but on the twenty-fifth, he noted that he "got a horse of Alexander Zachary and went as far as Mr. Wilson's on Cullowhee." Then, on the following day, he went on to John Messer's, sent the borrowed horse back to Zachary and, with another horse, borrowed this time from Messer, he managed to reach home in the night.

The following year, in July 1854, he made the entry in his diary, "Gave a subscription paper for the railroad to Woodford Zachary." Woodford, another of the brothers of Mordecai, ended up living in the East LaPorte area of Jackson County, where he married and raised a large family.

Not much has been found that connects Will Thomas and Cashiers Valley during the first half of the 1860s—those terrible years of the Civil War. Of course, Thomas was completely consumed with leading his storied Confederate Thomas Legion. Although no hard evidence has been located as proof, it is believed that Mordecai Zachary served in the legion and that his wife and children spent many of the war years with her own family in Quallatown.

This was a safer place in those years than was Cashiers Valley, where the threat of a raid by the Bushwhackers was always a constant danger. The carving on Mordecai's tombstone at the Whittier Cemetery does testify to his being part of the Thomas Legion. The only time Mordecai Zachary's name has thus far been found in the Thomas papers was in February 1866, when Thomas wrote:

> *Directed Mordecai Zachary to send an order to William Norton for a straw cutter that the said Zachary purchased of said William Norton for me for which he paid 100 in Treasury Notes.*

The war was over and Thomas was back at his farming duties.

Seven years after this straw cutter deal, and shortly after the death of his father, Mordecai Zachary sold his house and property in Cashiers Valley. It was 1873, and neither Mordecai nor his wife or children would ever again live in the valley where he had grown to manhood. The family moved to the area in northern Jackson County that would later be known as "Whittier." Proven by Jackson County deeds, his next-door neighbor was Will Thomas. Just a year after the move, the thirteenth and final child of Mordecai and Elvira was born at their new residence. It was a little girl named Hattie Sue, who lived a long life, not departing this earth until 1951 in Rosewood, California. Her descendants, as well as descendants of her siblings, tell this story of Hattie Sue Zachary and Will Thomas.

As a young child, she must have possessed some special abilities. After the end of the Civil War, which had completely drained Will Thomas and left him a broken old man with little prospects for a future, he was placed in a mental institution in Raleigh. He was released many times to return home, only to be returned again to the asylum. During the times he was back at his beloved mountain home and his wife would see a bad spell coming on, she would quickly send someone over to the Zachary house to bring back Hattie Sue. There was something in her young, pretty, innocent face and demeanor that had a calming effect on the old man, and Colonel Thomas would slowly return to normal.

BEFORE BARTRAM— 1767 JOURNEY OF THOMAS GRIFFITH

Today I want you to come along with me on a long-ago journey that was instigated by Josiah Wedgwood, the English founder of Wedgwood China. We'll see a glimpse of what life was like in colonial South Carolina and in the North Carolina mountain hunting grounds of the Cherokee Nation in the years 1767 and 1768. In 1766, Wedgwood obtained from a friend his first samples of white clay from the Carolinas. He had previously heard of a fine clay called Cherokee clay, or as he referred to it, "Cherokee Earth." Wedgwood's curiosity was so great that he became determined to obtain a quantity sample. He started an investigation to learn the exact location of the clay, and while on a visit to the House of Commons in London, he ascertained the correct name of the site and the exact location on a map, and he began looking into methods of communicating with that distant country and securing a right to its rich, alluvial deposits. He was advised to send an agent, without delay, to America, before his competitors beat him to it.

Now, let's bring today's main player onstage: Thomas Griffith, a fellow Brit who had spent some time in America and had a part interest in three thousand acres of land in South Carolina. He was described as both a geologist and botanist, as well as being a keen businessman. He certainly was possessed of an adventurous spirit. Josiah Wedgwood employed Griffith as his agent at fifty pounds per annum, plus expenses, and arranged for him to receive credit at a bank in Charleston. The voyage to America was to begin on the July 16, 1767.

So, nine years before William Bartram came through these mountains on his famous travels, Griffith set out from London on a ship, appropriately named *America*, on his own incredible journey. Much like Bartram, he methodically kept a day-by-day detailed journal of his quest, which took him to the same Cherokee Indian territory that Bartram later visited. The northernmost point of this trip was about eight miles north of today's town of Franklin in the general area of NC Highway 28, or the old road to Bryson City. The original of Griffith's diary is presently on display at the Wedgwood Museum in Barleston, England, but a copy can be found at the North Carolina Department of Archives and History in Raleigh.

A couple of decades back, Western Carolina University Professor William L. Anderson, using Griffith's diary, wrote a thirty-four-page article for the *North Carolina Historical Review*, entitled "'Cherokee Clay' from Duche to Wedgwood: The Journal of Thomas Griffith, 1767–1768." The greater part of my talk today is based on Dr. Anderson's well-researched article. As part of his journal, Griffith kept an account book in which he entered his expenditures and his receipts. An interesting entry was the payment for "Tea and Coffee for the journey," showing him to have the tastes of both an Englishman and an American.

The voyage across the Atlantic proved to be a shaky two-month sailing with at least one baby born in steerage. The ship *America* finally reached the Charles Town, South Carolina port on September 21, and Griffith wrote that they encountered there "a miserable hot and sickly time." In 1767, the port of Charles Town was a thriving city of about ten thousand inhabitants. It was one of the leading seaports engaged in trade with Great Britain, and in the English New World, Charles Town ranked second in the number of ships and seamen involved in commerce. The three leading goods sent from South Carolina to England were rice, indigo and hemp. There had been a brisk "skin trade" coming from South Carolina, but it had declined by 1767. In those days, the words "skin trade" referred to animal skins or pelts.

In order to get to the Cherokee clay, Griffith had to proceed through the Carolina backcountry, a region that began about fifty to sixty miles from the coast and extended to the mountain foothills. In the 1760s, this was extremely dangerous territory through which to travel. The Cherokee War had ended in 1761, barely five years before Thomas Griffith arrived. That war had devastated the Cherokees with so many of their villages burned. They were *not* feeling real good about *any* white man.

Another threat to the traveler were lawless individuals who had flooded the backcountry and seemed beyond the control of both Native American and white societies. They preyed on the frontier planters and on any travelers passing by. The South Carolina backcountry was almost completely lacking in a local government, leaving the honest man at the mercy of the unscrupulous. This was the gauntlet that Griffith had to run to reach his prize of the Cherokee clay. He actually did encounter some of the outlaws, but suffered no adverse effects—all duly noted in his journal.

After reaching Charleston, Griffith remained there for a number of days, finally heading north on Sunday, October 4. He wrote, "I am off for the Cherokee Nation." The first stage was Dorchester, twenty-five miles from Charleston. Northeast of Dorchester he encountered a troublesome, dangerous road that took him through two large swamps named Cypress and the Four Holes. He had gone fifty miles by the time he got through those hazards. He then observed people reaping fine rice on Captain Young's rice plantation with a "middling good tavern" located in the forks of the Edisto River. About this time, his horse fell lame, obliging him to travel more slowly and transfer his baggage to a wagon.

The next place he came to was Orangeburg, which

> *is a considerable large neighborhood and affords a tavern, a shop and a man that pretended to preach. Here my horse obliged me to stop two nights and then I proceeded for Indian Head, twenty miles west of Orangeburg.*

You'll realize this was a zigzag route, but Griffith had to follow the established roads, such as they were.

Next was Ridge Spring, about twenty miles east of Edgefield. Along the way to Ridge Spring, he briefly joined company with a trader, a meeting Griffith considered as lucky as it was "a thing very rare to see either person or so much as a poor hut while traveling through these woods." The two reached Ridge Spring, described as a small pleasant village and a tavern, but frequently visited by thieves. The trader remained in the village while Griffith continued on to Coffee Creek and made a stop at a tavern, where he observed that "here the people were all sick and lay about the room like dogs." He bought some corn for his horse and for himself potatoes, bread and a fowl. He slept part of the night under a pine tree.

The next day, Griffith marched on for Andrew Williamson's at Whitehall, near today's town of Ninety-Six, which was two hundred miles from Charleston. He wrote about the Whitehall Plantation:

This is one of the finest plantations in South Carolina with rich red loamy land, famous for raising corn, hemp, flax, cotton, rice, cattle, hogs, fruits of all sorts and a great plenty of mulberrys and peaches innumerable. The surrounding woods contained fine white and black oak, ash, maple, hickory, birch and many lofty pines.

On October 17, he left Whitehall with a Native American woman who belonged to the chiefs of the Cherokees and was on her way back to her original home. They proceeded on to Captain Aaron Smith's, located in today's Abbeville County on the Little River, where "we found middling good beds." The next two nights they were obliged to sleep in the woods.

Soon Griffith and the native woman got to Fort Prince George, near the Indian line. The fort had been constructed in 1753 and was built just across the Keowee River from the Cherokee settlement of Old Keowee. Today, Lake Keowee covers both the fort and the Native American settlement. At the fort, Griffith "delivered up my Squaw and letters to the commanding officer of that place who received me with much politeness. Here I also met with the Deputy Commissioner for Indian Affairs." While at the fort, Griffith met with several men of the Cherokee Nation. He named the following three: the great prince of Chotee, also called Kittagusta, who had been a chief during the recent Cherokee War; the old wolf of the Keowee, who was at that time the headman of Keowee; and Kinetita of Hiwassee. Then there were various young warriors and also the Great Bear, the Cherokee chief who was later succeeded by Yonoluska, the first chief of the eastern band of the Cherokee. These important Cherokee personages were in the middle of holding a council or a grand talk at the fort to agree on yet another peace treaty.

Griffith was able to eat, drink, smoke and become familiar with "these strange, copper colored gentry," and he quickly took this rare opportunity to formally request leave to travel through their country, "in search of anything that curiosity might lead me to, and in particular, to speculate on their Ayoree White Earth." The word *Ayoree* was the Cherokee name for the settlement and the mountain where the clay was located. The linguist translated Griffith's requests to the prestigious Cherokee group, and after a long hesitation and a debate among themselves, they granted the request. One Native American disliked the decision, saying that there had been trouble with some white men who made great holes in their land, took away their fine white clay and gave them only promises for it.

On October 30, Griffith took leave of the fort and proceeded for the Cherokee Middle Settlements and the mountains. He crossed the Chattooga

River and the Warwoman's Creek, which was a little east of today's Clayton, Georgia. Then he crossed the Six Dividers, which was a point in the road that contained six trails to various points of Cherokee territory.

He crossed a great number of small brooks and springs that run their course between the mountains. That night he wrote:

> *The Savannas are in some places very rotten and dangerous for strange travelers. In several parts a man and his horse may sink in fifteen or twenty feet and would unavoidably perish. I had but little time to stop as it was then that the Miserablest Weather I had ever been exposed to…A cold wind came from the Northeast with cold and heavy rain and sleet beginning at five in the morning and continuing until nine at night at which time I arrived at an Indian hut which was the first shelter I came upon. By that time there was scarce left in either me or my poor horse. When I went inside and advanced near the fire the weariness came over me and I fell down. Unluckily, the master had gone out, so I had no other refreshment than potatoes and bread and water and some Indian corn for my horse.*
>
> *The poor old squaw dried my clothes, as well as she could, and wrapped me up in a blanket and a bearskin. The next morning my night's landlord returned home and some fowls were stewed which made me a glorious repast. This being Sunday the first of November, I set off for Patrick Gallihorn's at Cowee Town on the Tennessee River.*

Two notes here: first, William Bartram also mentioned Patrick Gallihorn when he came by nine years later; and second, Cowee Town on the Tennessee River was actually a little distance beyond Griffith's destination of Ayoree, but Cowee Town was the largest of the Cherokee Middle Towns. It had a trading post, and thus supplies could be obtained there. Griffith wrote:

> *I remained here for a few days and furnished myself with a servant, tools, blankets and bearskins. On the 3 of November, we retired to Ayoree Mountain, where we remained until the 23rd of December.*

Those weeks proved to be a worrisome time for our adventurer. They first labored hard for three days in clearing away the rubbish out of the old pit. The rubbish added up to twelve or fifteen tons. On the fourth day, the pit was well cleared out and the clay appeared fine. But to Griffith's great surprise, the chief men of Ayoree came and took him prisoner, telling him he was a trespasser on their land. A linguist was found and with lengthy strong talk between Griffith and the Native Americans, an agreement was made—they shook hands—and it was back to digging. Four days of labor yielded one ton of clay ready for the pack horses, but the weather changed and such heavy rains fell that a torrent flowed from the upper mountains, not only filling the pit with water, but the clay that had already been dug was melted, stained with red mud and spoiled.

During the rest of the process of this work, the Native Americans often paid troublesome visits.

> *I invited them together and heated them with Rum and such music as I was capable of, which made them dance with great agility, especially when the bottle was about gone. This is the only way to make friendship with any Indians, provided they are not made drunk.*

By December 18, Griffith had dug and dried all the clay he intended to take, and as the pack horses were still at the fort, he had a few days to hunt, fossil and botanize. It was a hard winter for this part of the world—the Tennessee River often froze over and the food in the cook pot would almost freeze even over a slow fire. Griffith had never felt so cold in his life. He wrote:

> *On the 23rd of December, I took my leave of this cold and mountainous country and went off with the pack horses for Fort Prince George. But, with the frosty weather and the mountain paths being very narrow and slippery, we killed and spoiled some of the best horses and at last my own horse slipped down and rolled several times over me. I saved myself by laying hold of a young tree but the poor beast tumbled into a creek and was spoiled.*

On the twenty-seventh, he arrived again at Fort George, which was at that time a welcome prospect. "When I came up to the parade ground, I could have gladly kissed the Soldiers for joy." He remained there until January 14, 1768, at which time he loaded five wagons with the five tons of clay and set off for Charles Town. The light horses, bad roads and solid loading obliged Griffith to travel very slowly. On January 18, he reached Little River and stayed with Parson Hamerer, a Lutheran missionary to the Cherokee. Then it was on to Captain Smith's tavern and next to Matthew Edwards's at Long Canes in Abbeville County. Many times he stayed the night in the woods, sometimes in heavy rain. After passing Dorchester, he arrived on February 4 at "dear and long wished for Charles Town where there is both good religion and laws and the people are mostly true patriots and dear lovers of Liberty." He continued to praise the inhabitants of Charles Town, calling them careful and thrifty, and said that the merchants transacted their business very quick and discreet.

On March 4, Griffith bid farewell to Charles Town and set sail for London. The passage endured bad weather with contrary winds and storms that slowed the trip. On the second week out, a violent storm took away the ship's foresail and topmast, but they kept going, and on the April 16, Thomas Griffith left the ship at Graves End and continued to London by land. The round trip from London had lasted a total of nine months.

The cost of the entire expedition came to over £600. The clay, itself, did not reach Liverpool until October 1768, and it lay there in a warehouse for some time before Wedgwood could put it to use. He considered the Cherokee Earth of a very fine quality and he later used it in the jasper body he developed in 1774. The locating of good clay in Cornwall, plus the cost and difficulty of Griffith's trip and the impending American Revolutionary War, prevented Josiah Wedgwood from seeking and acquiring any more of the Cherokee clay.

Now, let us fast forward to the twentieth century. On June 12, 1950, on Highway 28, about eight miles from downtown Franklin, a historical marker was set up to indicate the area of the Cherokee clay pit. The marker reads, "Wedgwood Potteries, England, used several

A roadside state historical marker near Franklin, North Carolina, indicating the location of the Cherokee clay pit visited by Thomas Griffith in 1767. *Jane Gibson Nardy.*

tons of clay taken in 1767 from a nearby pit by Thomas Griffith, a South Carolina planter."

Fast forward again to April 22, 1968, when Sir John Wedgwood personally dedicated a bronze tablet presented to the City of Franklin by the City of Charlotte, in observance of Charlotte's bicentenary. The inscription on the tablet reads:

> *1768–1968, in Celebration of the Bicentenary of Charlotte, N.C., this plaque presented to Franklin, N.C. in recognition of its Cherokee Clay, first used by Josiah Wedgwood 200 years ago. Dedicated by his great-great-grandson, Sir John Wedgwood.*

This ceremony was just a part of the week-long Thirteenth Wedgwood International Seminar, which was being held in Charlotte in 1968 with 420 registrants attending. One of the field trips offered to the participants was to Franklin, a four-hour bus ride away. On the bus, excerpts from Griffith's diary were read. A short ride out to the clay pit was made, and many of the visitors dug up some white clay to take home.

In closing, I want to share an interesting bit of Josiah Wedgwood's genealogy. After his death in 1795, a large part of his estate went to his daughter, Susannah Wedgwood Darwin, whose son, Charles Darwin, would one day be even more renowned than his grandfather.

A PICTURE IS WORTH
A THOUSAND WORDS

O n August 20, 2007, the first copies of *Cashiers Valley* arrived at various stores and shops around town. *Cashiers Valley* is a pictorial history of Cashiers put together by Jan Blair Wyatt and yours truly and published by Arcadia. A few hours later, I saw Marilyn Staats at the library. I showed her the book, and after a quick look, Marilyn said, "Will you do a program for the Cashiers library about writing *Cashiers Valley*?" I agreed, but later, at home, I got to wondering what in the world I could say about a bunch of pictures with captions. I have heard many authors read paragraphs from their (usually fiction) books, but that wouldn't work with photographs. So I thought and thought and looked through the book a few more times—and it finally hit me. A lot of people can look at the same photo, but it will have a different meaning for each person. I started looking at the pictures with new eyes, and found in their depths all kinds of feelings and remembrances I could share with an audience. Following are those stories.

A great-uncle of mine, Roy Zachary, who left Cashiers in the early 1900s to work in Washington State, lived a life that has startled his descendants. As a child, I remember him on one of his visits back to the mountains. I sat on his shoulders while climbing Mount Pisgah. But most of all, I remember learning that in the 1930s, through to the end of World War II, my sweet Uncle Roy was a leading spokesman for the Silver Shirts, who were American Nazis. During the war, our government incarcerated him

Liberation

★★★ Facts Behind The Crisis ★★★

Chicago's Jews might read Thomas Paine: "Like men in a state of intoxication, you forget that the rest of the world has eyes and that the stupidity which conceals you from yourselves exposes you to its contempt!"

VOL. IX—No. 26   ASHEVILLE, N. C., NOVEMBER 28, 1938   PRICE 10 CENTS

ZACHARY IS SLUGGED IN JEW-PAID TERRORISM

THUGGERY and terrorism now come to the aid of Jewry! The place is Chicago. The time is our most recent Thanksgiving Week.

Among the victims of premeditated Jewish terrorism was Field Marshal Roy Zachary of the Silvershirt Legion, bludgeoned from all sides and felled because he had the courage to speak out against Jews from the platform!

While our provenly-Jewish President is sending quips of disgusting blah across the radio from his Thanksgiving table — about how close and touching is the friendship between the smutty-joke-telling Eddie Cantor and himself—scenes of different import are being enacted in Chicago!

Chicago Jews, failing in all other expedients to halt Silvershirts in exercise of their constitutional right of free speech, are employing or fomenting bodies of Jewish sluggers to crash meetings, break skulls, wreck property, and send police and audience to hospitals!

By such tactics does this "defenseless and persecuted minority" bethink to destroy and crush opponents of its anti-Christian usurpations.

Three riots in seven days, involving Silvershirts, spectators, and policemen, is the record distinguishing this last week of November. Fifteen men in all have been jailed. Three are in the hospital.

Roy Zachary, Field Marshal for the Silvershirts, was bludgeoned and bruised so badly that seven stitches were taken in his scalp.

The November 28, 1938 front page of *Liberation*, a pro-Nazi journal printed by William Dudley Pelley in Asheville, North Carolina. Roy Zachary became Pelley's associate. *Jane Gibson Nardy.*

somewhere in the Midwest to keep a close eye on him. Oh, what a mixed bag of kinfolk I have!

My great-step-grandmother in Cashiers was referred to as "Aunt Mary" by one and all. She was the second wife of my great-grandfather, T.R. Zachary. Walter Taylor of Highlands, who often wears kilts and gives talks on the Scots-Irish mountain people, told me that "Aunt Mary" Rogers Zachary was also his aunt through the Rogers line. In 1927, Aunt Mary traveled with some of her family to New York State to visit relatives. She stayed at the home of Walter Taylor's parents. Walter was just a few years old and was having a bad case of the "croup," with phlegm filling his throat and choking off his breathing. Aunt Mary asked, "Is there any whiskey in the house?" A bottle was produced and a shot was poured down Walter's throat, which resulted in opening up his airway. "Aunt Mary literally saved my life," Walter said.

Citizens of both Highlands and Cashiers claim Whiteside Mountain as their town's mountain. I think it is big enough to go around, don't you? As Robert Zahner told us in his book, *The Mountain at the End of the Trail*, published in 1994, a group of professionals and businessmen from Highlands and Cashiers in 1950 formed a corporation to turn Whiteside Mountain into a commercial enterprise. The president of this new firm was W. Frank Lewis, manager of High Hampton Inn in Cashiers. The plan was to make Whiteside rival Chattanooga's famed Rock City. In 1948, the Powell brothers, who owned Whiteside, sold the mountain to Whiteside Mountain, Inc. Today, the very thought of private ownership of Whiteside is unseemly.

A road was built to provide automobile access to the top of Whiteside. A tram car with seats for passengers was pulled by a jeep to the top. A ten-by-ten wooden platform, fifteen feet high, was built near the summit, providing a 360-degree view. A 1950 news release about the view from this platform proclaimed, "Looking down off Whiteside one feels as if he is on the pinnacle of the universe and is viewing the rest of the world in miniature."

At the entrance from Highway 64 was a huge log gateway with a tollhouse where fees were collected. Two men served as attendants, one at the highway where a dollar per person was charged as a toll for the drive up the mountain, and another at the parking area where twenty-five cents was charged for the tram ride to the summit. A concession stand sold soft drinks, candy bars and hot dogs.

What I remember most about that short commercial venture was a local old man who often stood on top of the fifteen-foot platform to answer questions. One visitor said, "The signs say 'See four states from the top of Whiteside Mountain.' What are the four states?"

The old man scratched his head and answered, "North Carolina and South Carolina and Georgia, and…well, I guess Texas." Those of you who have not read *The Mountain at the End of the Trail*, should do so. But be warned—you're likely to cry.

Every year, Halloween comes. And every year we need a ghost story. Hannibal Heaton and his wife, Louisa Emmalie Zachary are the subjects of Cashiers's best-known ghost story. The story is often incorrect, as you have read in the previous section "Cashiers Ghost Buster." I want to tell you how I got some wonderful pictures of Hannibal, Emmalie and their family. Through the Internet, I was contacted a few years ago by a lady named Barbara Chambless of Las Vegas. She was a descendant of the Zachary family of Cashiers and was interested in the family tree. As it turned out, her great-grandparents were Hannibal Heaton and Emmalie Zachary.

Barbara had inherited her grandmother's cedar chest, which, much to her surprise, was filled with Zachary and Heaton memorabilia, including pictures over 135 years old that had been made on glass negatives. Old documents found in the chest indicated that prior to her post–Civil War marriage to Hannibal Heaton, Emmalie Zachary was first married in 1862, at age sixteen, to a Jackson County young man named Francis Marion Moody, who served in the Union army until his death. A few pages of Civil War pension applications in the name of Hannibal Heaton, who also served as a Union soldier, were in the trunk. One of his daughters, who was a minor when he died, also had applied, after Hannibal's death, for a pension on her father's service. I ordered full copies of these pensions and they totaled over one hundred pages. The pension office needed proof that Emmalie's first husband was dead before she married Hannibal, so copies of wartime letters from Francis Moody to Emmalie and affidavits from fellow soldiers who saw Moody fatally shot and buried on the grounds of Mars Hill College were included in the pension files.

The contents of that cedar chest provided a description from about 1862 to their deaths of the often tragic lives of Emmalie Zachary Moody Heaton and her two husbands, Francis Marion Moody and Hannibal Heaton. Once again, the truth was scarier, by far, than the ghost story.

There is an old road, from the earliest days of Cashiers, that is now a hiking trail on High Hampton property, and that road brings back a clear childhood memory for me. The banks of the old road are rather high, clearly showing its age. From my great-grandfather's house, where we usually stayed when we were in town, it was but a short walk to the old road that led to the Upper Zachary Cemetery. At various places on the road banks were extensive outcroppings of what we called isinglass. We weren't aware of the word "mica." There were great quantities of the stuff we could peel off in large, thin pieces, some as big as a car window. It reminds me of the lyrics to an old song that describes a car "with Isinglass curtains you can roll right down in case there's a change in the weather." Today, there's not a single sighting of isinglass to be seen on that old road, due perhaps to the prying hands of many children just like me.

A friend of mine in Cashiers, by the name of Carolyn O'Leary, told me a good story about the late General William Westmoreland. About six years ago, Kitsey Westmoreland, wife of the general, hired Carolyn as a housekeeper.

The first day that Carolyn arrived at the Westmoreland home in the High Hampton Colony, she was greeted by Kitsey, who said that the general had gone to play golf with some friends, and after showing Carolyn where she should start working, Kitsey left for an appointment with the hairdresser. Just before leaving, Kitsey said, "If I'm not back by the time the general returns, just introduce yourself."

After a couple of hours had passed, Carolyn had just finished mopping the kitchen floor when she looked up and saw General Westmoreland, with shoes dirty from the golf course, walking toward the kitchen door. Carolyn opened the door and said, "Stop, general, you can't come in this door."

The general, looking surprised and a little miffed, answered, "What do you mean I can't come in this door? Do you know who I am?"

Without missing a beat, Carolyn said, "Yes I know who you are, you're General Westmoreland, but I just mopped the kitchen floor, so please use the front door." What an introduction.

Some of you might have wondered how Jan and I came to write *Cashiers Valley*. It is quite simple. Someone at Arcadia Publishing realized that neither Cashiers nor Highlands had yet been tapped for a pictorial history. They called the Cashiers Historical Society for help in finding an author or authors. Jan heard about it and called me to see if I would help her with the project. I balked at first, but Jan is persuasive, so we signed the contract. That was well over a year ago.

A few months before the book was due to be released, Jan and her husband made the decision to relocate to Louisiana, where her son and some grandchildren live. By the time the book hit the stores, Jan was long gone and I thought I was left holding the bag. I soon realized that instead of the bag, it was the glory I was left with. *Cashiers Valley* is proving to be popular.

Uncle Alton Demar "Tete" Bowers in his heyday in the 1930s. He attempted liberties with his nieces and was punished for it after his death. *Geneva Zachary Gibson.*

My mother, Geneva Zachary, posed for a picture in the 1920s, with Whiteside Mountain behind her and the Devil's Courthouse clearly visible. She was about eighteen years old and was sitting on a split rail fence located on the dirt road to her grandfather, T.R. Zachary's, house. This was a time period before the logging of Whiteside Mountain took place. If only we had a close-up of that photo, we could see living chestnut trees and some of the primeval hardwood trees still standing. What a treat that would be.

Geneva's father, John A. Zachary, graduated from Teachers Normal in Cullowhee in 1899. This school was the forerunner of Western Carolina University. In 1900, he went to Georgia to teach school in a one-room schoolhouse—grades one through twelve. There he met Viola Crossley. They married in 1904, and Geneva was born in Atlanta in 1906. At an early age, she started coming to Cashiers for the summer where she always stayed with her grandparents. The trip from Atlanta to Cashiers began at the Terminal Train Station in downtown Atlanta, and continued on the train to Hendersonville, where one changed to the train that went to Toxaway, which was the end of the line. There at the Toxaway train station, T.R. Zachary would be waiting with his horse and wagon for his granddaughter. Geneva would hop in the wagon with her suitcase and off they would ride, slowly making the last leg of the journey up the mountains to Cashiers Valley. Often they had to get out and remove large boulders that were blocking the road.

Geneva spent the summer roaming the valley with her cousins and friends, eating food produced at her grandfather's farm, helping to churn the butter, carry water from the spring and milk the cows. All of this was pure heaven for Geneva—she loved everything about Cashiers and continued to feel that way her entire life. She brainwashed me and my sister into thinking the same way.

Julia Luckie Zachary, Geneva's younger sister, was a redheaded star of the flapper age. She went through school, both grammar school and high school, with a sweetheart named Alton Demar Bowers. Everyone called him by his nickname, "Tete." Sometimes he reminded us of a short Clark Gable, but at other times he looked like "Mo" of the *Three Stooges*. He dropped out of school without graduating, but then, he was never known for his intelligence. After Julia graduated, the two were married.

Tete worked in a machine shop, Julia was the vice-president of a candy company and they never had children. We lived a few minutes' walk from them, and my sister and I were the closest thing they had to children.

My sister, June, who was six years my elder, suffered a crude attempt at groping from Uncle Tete when she was just age thirteen. She never told anyone until she was grown, so I was not pre-warned. I was sixteen when Uncle Tete drove me to a drive-in beer joint, where he ordered a beer for himself and a soft drink for me. Then his hand slithered over to my thigh. I removed his hand and told him I didn't need him to be a boyfriend, but just needed him to be an uncle. It worked. He left me alone.

When Julia died at the young age of fifty-six, Tete continued living in their home. Julia's mother, my Granny, had lived with them for many years and a lot of her belongings were still in the house—all sorts of Zachary family memorabilia like photograph albums, silver serving dishes engraved with the letter "Z" and T.R. Zachary's chifforobe and mustache cup. My mother wrote to Tete asking him to return the items. He responded by coming to her house, throwing the family photographs on the doorstep and telling Mother and Granny that if they wrote him another "g— d—" letter he would kill them both and burn their house down.

The next day, while visiting with Granny, she asked me to promise her that when Tete died, he would not be buried in her plot in the cemetery, although Julia had been buried there. Granny said, "I don't want to lie through eternity in the same grave plot with that man." I got her in my car, we drove to the Oakland cemetery office and we had the ownership of the plot changed from her name to my name with instructions not to allow anyone to be buried there without my permission.

A few years later, Granny died at age eighty-seven and was buried between her husband, John Zachary, and her daughter, Julia. Years passed, and on one of my visits to the cemetery, much to my shock, there was a new tombstone with Tete's name on it. His second wife had buried him there, without anyone's permission. Boy was I mad. I rushed to the cemetery office. They checked the records and apologized for their mistake. I said, "I want him out of there—now." They gave me his widow's phone number. I rushed to Mother's and told her what happened. She looked at me with sad eyes and said, "Oh, Jane, don't do that, he was a fool but Julia loved him."

It took a while, but justice for Granny was finally achieved. My sister went in with me, and we had a footstone carved and placed at the bottom of Tete's grave. It says, "He was a fool but Julia loved him. Quote Geneva Zachary Gibson." It is true that revenge is a dish best served cold. Granny would approve of the fact that, although Tete was in her plot, he would lie there through eternity identified as a fool.

A group of "Scottish Laddies," were hired by the Wade Hampton Golf Course, straight from Scotland, to serve as caddies. A few of them lived in my sister's cabin, "Birdsnest," during their stay. They were young college-age boys, and for most, it was their first visit to the United States.

The size of this country left them dumbfounded. They thought they could go from Cashiers to the beach and back in a day. They had no conception of the distance to California. The ones staying in my sister's cabin had too much to drink one night and ended up getting into a big fight in the middle of Monte Vista Road. Neighbors saw them hitting each other and rolling in a ditch. Needless to say, the police were called. The laddies did not return to Cashiers the next year.

T.R. Zachary was born in Cashiers Valley in 1850. In 1864, at age fourteen, he guided a group of escaped Union army soldiers from Cashiers to safety in Knoxville. There is much more to his life story of interest. He was quite an adventurer.

By the time he was twenty years old, he was living on the American frontier in Kansas, with his brother, Christopher Columbus Zachary. T.R. went back and forth from Cashiers to Kansas over the period of a few years, and while he was back East, he met his wife-to-be while peddling seeds and seedlings to farmers in Georgia. He returned to Kansas and decided to homestead in the western part of that state, so he staked a claim, built himself a little soddy house, planted trees as a windbreak, prepared the earth for farming and, through the mail, he courted his Georgia sweetheart. Most of those letters have survived. T.R. and his sweetheart were finally married in 1879, and she joined him in Kansas. Life was hard on the frontier and T.R. had to sometimes work for a few months as a laborer, helping to build the railroad going farther west. His first child was born in Kansas in 1881, but soon after, the family returned to Cashiers Valley, where they would remain for the rest of their lives.

I am going to finish up with something very interesting that you can see on the face of Rock Mountain—it is now called the rainbow-shaped crack. The mountains that stand guard over Cashiers Valley are Whiteside, Chimney Top and Rock Mountain. Their silhouettes and faces are as familiar to us as our own. The experts tell us these mountains are among the oldest in the world, and we imagine their creation in volcanic bursts, the great heights they once attained and their eons-long weathering that wore them down to what we know today—smaller, but still majestic in their decline. But wait, Rock Mountain, only 121 years ago, underwent a violent face-changing experience that some claim originated in the Atlantic Ocean.

An oil painting of Rock Mountain and the rainbow crack as seen from High Hampton Inn in Cashiers. *Artist Button Parham.*

On August 31, 1886, at approximately 9:50 p.m. and lasting for about one minute, the most damaging earthquake to ever occur in the Southeastern United States struck the city of Charleston, South Carolina, leaving much of that lovely place a heap of rubble. The shock waves continued on, racing west–northwest, and when those waves encountered Cashiers Valley's Rock Mountain, a huge rainbow-shaped crack, one hundred yards wide and twelve feet deep, appeared two-thirds of the way down from the top of the mountain. Because this event took place prior to today's precise seismological instrumentation, estimates of its location and size must come from observations of the damage and effects caused by the quake. Most agree that it would have been a number seven on the Richter scale.

Effects were felt and structural damage was reported from central Alabama, central Ohio, eastern Kentucky, North Carolina, southern Virginia and western West Virginia. It was felt as far away as Boston to the north, Chicago and Milwaukee to the northwest, as far west as New Orleans, as far south as Cuba and as far east as Bermuda. There were many aftershocks following the initial quake, as evidenced in the Highlands newspaper entitled the *Highlander*:

Friday, Sept. 3, 1886
Tuesday night was a beautiful one, brightly starlit and perfectly still.
Many Persons, finding their homes shaking in a decidedly unpleasant
manner, went out of doors to see what the matter was. It [the initial
earthquake] *was presently followed by slighter shocks at gradually*
lengthening intervals; one of these was felt as late as 3 o'clock
Wednesday morning.
As far as we can learn, this is the first time within memories of dwellers in
this part of the mountain country that it has been visited by earthquakes.

Friday, Sept. 19, 1886
Slight tremors have been felt here we believe, almost every night since the
heavier shocks of August 31.

Friday, Oct. 29, 1886
The courthouse at Walhalla was cracked in several places by Friday's
(Oct. 22) earthquake.

According to *Wikipedia*, "more than 300 aftershocks of the 1886
earthquake occurred within thirty-five years." The historic records suggest
that low-level activity, stemming from that late summer earthquake of
1886, can sometimes still be felt. Rock Mountain remembers.

SOURCES

Alley, Howard Eugene. *Presumed Dead: A Civil War Mystery*. Fairview, NC: Historical Images, 2002.

Biddix, Charles David, ed. *1835 Poll Books of North Carolina*. Asheville, NC: Old Buncombe County Genealogical Society, Inc., n.d.

Godbold, Dr. E. Stanly, and Mattie Russell. *Confederate Colonel, Cherokee Chief: The Life of William Thomas*. Knoxville: University of Tennessee Press, 1990.

Law, S. Van Epp. *Status Quo*. Stuart, FL: Southeastern Printing, Co., 1971.

Laws of the State of North Carolina, Passed by the General Assembly, At the Session of 1850–51. Raleigh, NC: T.J. Lemay, State Printer, 1851.

Leary, Helen F.M., and Maurice R. Stirewalt, eds. *North Carolina Research, Genealogy and Local History*. Raleigh: North Carolina Genealogical Society Inc., 1980.

Lombard, Frances Baumgarner. *From the Hills of Home in Western North Carolina*. N.p., n.d.

Marett, Bill. *Courage at Fool's Rock*. Highlands, NC: self-published, 1975.

Nardy, Jane Gibson. *The Cashiers Area—Yesterday, Today and Forever*. Dallas, TX: Taylor Publishing Co., 1994. Reprint, Charleston, SC: Arcadia Publishing, 2007.

Picklesimer, Thomas Eugene. *My Life and Times*. N.p., n.d.

Powell, William S. "Thomas Griffiths, A Journal of a Visit to the Cherokees, 1767." Unpublished ms., Raleigh, North Carolina State Library, n.d.

Russell, Randy, and Janet Barnett. *Mountain Ghost Stories*. Winston-Salem, NC: John R. Blair, Publisher, 1988.

Shaffner, Randolph P. *Heart of the Blue Ridge, Highlands, North Carolina*. Highlands, NC: Faraway Publishing, 2001.

Shelton, W.H. "A Hard Road to Travel, Out of Dixie." *Famous Adventures and Prison Escapes of the Civil War*. New York: Century Co., 1917.

Williams, Max R., ed. *The History of Jackson County*. Sylva, NC: Jackson County Historical Association, 1987.

Zahner, Robert. *The Mountain at the End of the Trail: A History of Whiteside Mountain*. Highlands, NC: self-published, 1994.

ABOUT THE AUTHOR

Jane Gibson Nardy lives in Cashiers on land that has been in her Zachary family since the 1830s. Her two daughters, son-in-law and two grandchildren are her nearest neighbors. She is related to an unknown number of residents in Cashiers and Highlands and frequently finds new cousins.

Jane serves as the historian for the Cashiers Historical Society. She is a guide at the Zachary-Tolbert House and leads two tours a year to explore Cashiers history sites. She was voted Volunteer of the Year for 2007 by the Cashiers Area Chamber of Commerce for her constant interest in preserving the history of the people and places of Cashiers.

Previous publications include *Cashiers Valley: A Pictorial History*, which she coauthored with Jan Blair Wyatt in 2007. In 1994, she led the Cashiers Area Chamber of Commerce publication of *The Cashiers Area—Yesterday, Today and Forever.* The *Encyclopedia of Appalachia*, published in 2006, contains an article on early mountain tourism, written by Jane. Since 2005, she has contributed a monthly Cashiers history article to the *Laurel* magazine.

If you have some old area photographs or know a good story, Jane would love to hear from you. Call her at 828-743-9002 or email janesaerie@aol.com.

Visit us at
www.historypress.net